Ernest Clarke

Eyestrain

Ernest Clarke

Eyestrain

ISBN/EAN: 9783744692434

Printed in Europe, USA, Canada, Australia, Japan

Cover: Foto ©ninafisch / pixelio.de

More available books at **www.hansebooks.com**

EYESTRAIN

(ASTHENOPIA)

BY

ERNEST CLARKE, M.D., B.S., (Lond.)

FELLOW OF THE ROYAL COLLEGE OF SURGEONS; SURGEON TO THE CENTRAL LONDON
OPHTHALMIC HOSPITAL; AND OPHTHALMIC SURGEON TO THE
MILLER HOSPITAL, ETC.

SECOND EDITION

London
J. & A. CHURCHILL
GREAT MARLBOROUGH STREET

BY THE SAME AUTHOR.

Haab's Atlas of Ophthalmoscopy and Ophthalmoscopic Diagnosis.

TRANSLATED AND EDITED BY

ERNEST CLARKE, M.D.Lond., F.R.C.S.

OPINIONS OF THE PRESS.

"The forms of disease selected to be illustrated, and the special cases depicted, are those that are most common and are likely to be most serviceable to the practitioner as types. Dr. ERNEST CLARKE may be congratulated as having translated a very useful work."—*Lancet*, December 7th, 1895.

"The translation appears to be well and carefully done, and to be free from German idiom. A great advantage of the atlas is its handiness."—*British Medical Journal*, July 11th, 1896.

"So far as Ophthalmological literature is concerned this volume marks an epoch worthy of special notice. The translator and editor, Dr. ERNEST CLARKE, has done his work well, and the book is worthy of the highest commendation."—*Medical Press and Circular*, February 26th, 1896.

London:
BAILLIÈRE, TINDALL & COX, KING WILLIAM ST., STRAND.

PREFACE TO THE SECOND EDITION.

THE only change made in this New Edition is the addition of a Short Appendix containing Abstracts of Papers read by me during the last four years, and bearing upon the subject of Eyestrain.

ERNEST CLARKE.

3, *Chandos Street,*
    Cavendish Square, W.

PREFACE TO FIRST EDITION.

A paper read by me before the West Kent Medico-Chirurgical Society in 1889, on "Ocular Headache," forms the framework upon which the following pages have been built.

The subject of Eyestrain has been very briefly dealt with in ophthalmic text books, and most of our knowledge of it is to be found in the scattered articles and papers by various authors, in the reviews and transactions of Societies, that have appeared from time to time.

The subject of Refraction is so intimately associated with Eyestrain that it has been found impossible, in many cases, to avoid referring to it in detail.

I must express my thanks to the many authors whose works have been consulted, but my greatest debt is due to the classical treatises of Donders and Landolt.

ERNEST CLARKE.

TABLE OF CONTENTS.

PART I.—EYESTRAIN.

GENERAL CONSIDERATIONS.

	PAGE
SECTION I.—History. Definition. The Varieties of Eyestrain	1
II.—General Symptoms. Pain. Ocular Pain	7
III.—Ocular Headache. Position. Frequency of Occurrence. Ætiology	9
IV.—Vertigo. Sickness. Diplopia. Unfamiliar Retinal Confusion. Insomnia	17
V.—Relations between Eyestrain and Severe Neuroses	21
VI.—Relative Frequency of Eyestrain	25
VII.—Differential Diagnosis of Eyestrain	30

PART II.—CILIARY STRAIN.

SECTION I.—Table of Causes	35
II.—Ciliary Strain in Emmetropia. Children's Work. Strain in Old Age; in Debility	35
III.—Neurasthenic Asthenopia	38
IV.—Strain in Anæmia, Constipation, Adolescence. Congenital Defect	40
V.—Reflex Asthenopia	41
VI.—Treatment of Ciliary Strain in Emmetropia. Hygiene of the Schoolroom. Testing the Sight. Shadow Test. Constitutional Treatment	43
VII.—Ciliary Strain in Ametropia	51
VIII.—Accommodation. Anatomical and Physiological Considerations. Amplitude of Accommodation	52
IX.—Influence of Age upon Accommodation. Presbyopia. Climacteric. Treatment	56
X.—Hyperopia. Varieties. Frequency. As a Cause of Eyestrain. Association between Accommodation and Convergence. Manifest, Latent and Facultative Hyperopia. Treatment	66

viii. *Table of Contents.*

	PAGE
SECTION XI.—Astigmatism. Varieties. Relative Frequency of Asthenopia in Astigmatism. How Caused. Treatment	79
XII.—Anisometropia. Varieties. Binocular Vision. Treatment	89

PART III.—MUSCULAR ASTHENOPIA.

SECTION I.—Anatomical and Physiological Considerations. ..	97
II.—Relation of the two Eyes to each other in Normal Vision. Test for Latent Deviation (distance)...	103
III.—Convergence. Nagel's Metre-Angle. Amplitude of Convergence. Test for Latent Deviation (near vision). Relation between Accommodation and Convergence. Fusion Supplement	105
IV.—Muscular Insufficiency. Definition. Heterophoria. Exophoria. Convergence Insufficiency. Esophoria. Hyperphoria. Insufficiency of the Obliques	115
V.—Table of Causes of Muscular Asthenopia ...	126
VI.—Muscular Asthenopia in Emmetropia. Neurasthenic Asthenopia. Treatment	127
VII.—Muscular Asthenopia in Ametropia; in Hyperopia. Treatment	130
VIII.—In Myopia. The Myopic Eye. Treatment ...	131
IX.—In Astigmatism and Anisometropia	136
X.—Prisms. Decentering Lenses	137
XI.—Tenotomy for the Relief of Muscular Asthenopia	140
XII.—Recapitulation	145

PART IV.—RETINAL ASTHENOPIA.

SECTION I.—Physiological Considerations	151
II.—Symptoms	153
III.—Table of Causes	155
IV.—Retinal Strain from Abuse. Neurasthenic Retinal Asthenopia. Reflex Amblyopia ...	155
V.—Sun-blindness. Night-blindness	157
VI.—Snow-blindness	158
VII.—Electric Light-blindness	159
VIII.—Lightning-blindness	161
IX.—Erythropsia...	161
X.—Treatment	162
NOTE: On the Centering of Glasses	163

PART I.

THE HISTORY, DEFINITION, AND SYMPTOMS OF EYESTRAIN.

THE HISTORY, DEFINITION, AND SYMPTOMS OF EYE-STRAIN.

I. HISTORY.—As long ago as 1766 Taylor wrote a graphic sketch of asthenopia, which he styled "debilitas visus;" he confused the phenomena with those of amblyopia, and referred the complaint to some affection of the retina or choroid.[1] In 1816 Scarpa alludes to "Debollezza di vista per stanchezza di nervi," *i.e.*, weakness of vision from fatigue of the nerves.[2] In 1817 Beer calls it "amblyopia nervosa."[3] In 1840 Tyrrell vaguely refers to "impaired vision;" he considers it due to temporary congestion of the choroid, and if neglected, liable to pass into chronic choroiditis.[4] In 1841 Laurence calls it an "affection of the retina from excessive employment."[5] In the same year Bonnet and Pétrequin exclude the retina, and refer the primary cause of asthenopia to the muscular apparatus of the eye, attributing the disorder to a morbid activity of the muscles of the eyeball.[6] Again, in the same year, Adams calls the disease "muscular amaurosis," and says that "it depends upon the bending or partial folding and com-

---

[1] *Nova Nosographia Ophthalmica*, p. 151.
[2] *Trattato delle principale Malattie degli Occhi*, vol. ii., p. 241.
[3] *Lehre von den Augenkrankheiten*, vol. ii., p. 34.
[4] "Diseases of the Eye," vol. ii., p. 25.
[5] "Diseases of the Eye," p. 566.
[6] *Annal. d'Ocul.*, tome v., p. 250.

pression of the optic nerves, caused by the shortening and thickening of the recti muscles during a state of morbid contraction, which, farther, may be attributed to an affection of the third and sixth nerves, probably at or near to their origin."[1]

Later, Mackenzie says asthenopia is "that state of vision in which the eyes are unable to sustain any continued exercise upon near objects, although the patient, on first viewing such objects, generally sees them distinctly, although he can employ his sight for any length of time in viewing distant objects, and although the eyes appear sound,"[2] he attacks the different writers quoted above and disposes of their theories. He comes very near the truth when he says: "If the external muscles of the eyeball are in part the seat of the morbid condition upon which asthenopia depends, it is probable that they contribute to the disorder by their inability to continue the aid which they afford in their healthy state towards the adjustment of the eye to the vision of near objects. This adjustment evidently fails in the disease under consideration."[3] Through his ignorance of the ciliary muscle and its action, he thinks the adjustment is performed by the recti and obliqui compressing the eyeball, and so carrying the lens forward, while the distance between the retina and cornea is maintained. He considers the above theory much more probable and satisfactory than that of ascribing to the muscles a state of spasm, and yet, notwithstanding this, he expresses himself in favour of dividing the recti and

---

[1] "New Operation for the Cure of Amaurosis, Impaired Vision, and Short-sightedness," p. 12.
[2] "Asthenopia, or Weak-sightedness," *Edin. Med. and Surg. Journal*, No. 156, p. 3.
[3] *Ibid.*, p. 25.

obliqui, as performed and recommended by Guerin, Cunier, Adams and Bonnet.

Rightly did Donders say that this was a sad era in ophthalmic surgery, illustrating well that the gravest errors in treatment are mostly due to ignorance of the cause and pathology of a disease. Mackenzie took such an alarming view of the prognosis of asthenopia that he says:—

> "In many cases it is our duty to declare the disease incurable, and to explain to the patient and his friends that all that can be done for it, is as much as possible to save the sight. If the patient is a young lad bound apprentice to a sedentary trade . . . we must advise him to turn shop-keeper, or to apply himself to country work; if a female occupied constantly in sewing, to engage in household affairs or any other healthy active employment. Many a poor man have I told to give up his sedentary trade, and drive a horse and cart; while to those in better circumstances, and not far advanced in life, I have recommended emigration, telling them that though they never could employ their eyes advantageously in reading and writing, they might see sufficiently to follow the pastoral pursuits of an Australian colonist."[1]

At last, in 1858, Donders of Utrecht came to the rescue, and pointed out that the cause of asthenopia was hypermetropia,[2] and in his classical treatise on refraction published a few years later, he propounded his theory at considerable length. He says: "I have already asserted that hypermetropia is usually at the bottom of asthenopia. The truth of this assertion has been doubted. I now go a step further, and venture to maintain that in the pure form of asthenopia, hypermetropia is scarcely ever wanting."[3]

About the same time V. Graefe drew attention to the strain of the internal recti, which he called asthenopia

---

[1] *Op. cit.*, p. 25.
[2] *Nederlandsch Tijdschrift voor Geneesk*, p. 473.
[3] "The Accommodation and Refraction of the Eye," New Sydenham Society, 1864, p. 261.

muscularis,[1] and a little later in his memorable paper on the subject, says:—"Eine andere Quelle der asthenopie ist ganz unabhängig von der accomodationsarbeit und liegt in dem Spannungsverhältnissen der inneren Augenmuskeln."[2]

This period marks the final epoch in the history of asthenopia, for these two pioneers, Donders and Graefe, steered ophthalmologists into the proper channels of inquiry and investigation, and although naturally our knowledge of the subject has increased during the last thirty years, it has not materially altered.

Definition.—Asthenopia ("A, privative, $\sigma\theta\acute{\epsilon}\nu o \varsigma$, strength, ὤψ, eye) or eyestrain, is a symptom or group of symptoms, the result of straining some part of the eye apparatus. It has been defined as *weak sight*. This is wrong, as weakness is no more a necessary feature than it is in any other form of fatigue. Tired sight it may be called, but *not* weak sight. The word "asthenopia" is the cause of this faulty definition; but we cannot afford to discard it, for although the word "eyestrain" in many respects is preferable—carrying with it as it does its own definition, and implying no theory—it does not supply us with an adjective, and the word "asthenopic" is very useful.

The Varieties of Eyestrain.—Eyestrain arises from strain of three distinct parts of the eye apparatus:—

(i.) Ciliary strain, commonly called accommodative asthenopia, due to strain of the ciliary muscle.

(ii.) Muscular asthenopia, due to strain of the extrinsic muscles of the eye; strain of the internal recti, or *convergence strain*, being the commonest form.

---

[1] Graefe's *Arch. f. Oph.*, bd. ii., 1, p. 174.
[2] *Ibid.*, bd. viii., 2., p. 321.

(iii.) Retinal asthenopia, due to strain of the retina and its connections.

II. **GENERAL SYMPTOMS.**—I cannot do better than quote the words used by Tyrrell fifty years ago, when writing on "impaired vision." He says: "Usually in the commencement of this affection, after the eyes have been engaged for some time on minute objects, the patient experiences a degree of confusion, the objects becoming partly or wholly obscured as if covered by a network or mist; but after resting the eyes for a few moments, and rubbing or pressing them slightly, the vision again becomes distinct; this occurs again and again, and the disturbance of vision is excited more readily and more rapidly the more the vision is exerted, and a longer period of rest is required for the subsidence of the effect, in proportion as the rapidity of the effect is produced. After some time a slight attempt to view minute objects reinduces the obscurity, and eventually the vision remains cloudy or dull, as if a piece of gauze or a thick veil intervened between the eye and the objects regarded. This condition . . . is usually attended by a sense of fulness in the eyeball, and a weight or uneasiness about the forehead."[1] At the same time the eyes appear perfectly normal, their movements undisturbed, and vision acute. At first, distant vision is as good as ever, but when the disease has lasted some time that even fails. Headache is a very common symptom; it is generally frontal, and more especially limited to the brows, but it may pass to the vertex and occiput, and even down the spine; it may be accompanied by a feeling of sickness, dyspepsia, vomiting, diplopia, vertigo and palpitation; insomnia has often been traced to it. The feeling of tension or fulness in the eyes may become real pain of

---

[1] *Op. cit.*, vol. ii., p. 26.

a dull aching character, and the eyeballs may be tender to pressure. Although at first there is no sign of inflammation or congestion in the eyes, if the eyestrain remains unrelieved they will appear, and we observe all the symptoms of conjunctivitis; the patient suffers from red, irritable and watery eyes, and the papillæ hypertrophy, producing "granular lids," which disease reacts upon and increases the irritability of the eyes. Blepharitis and other lid troubles follow in the train, and the optic disc has been seen congested and even swollen.

Harper relates three cases of severe conjunctival and corneal inflammation due to strain caused by hyperopic astigmatism, all cured by correcting glasses.[1]

Lippincott records two cases of muscular asthenopia, in which there was a sharply defined redness, resembling episcleritis, over the insertion of the internal recti muscles.[2]

Pain.—When this is the result of eyestrain it is of the non-inflammatory kind (unless the symptoms have passed on to actual inflammation, such as conjunctivitis), and is always brought on or exaggerated by the use of the eyes. It may be located in and entirely limited to the eyes themselves, or more generally, it may spread to the neighbouring parts, or it may originate in the head as a headache.

Ocular Pain.—Pain is almost too strong a word to use for the discomfort produced by strain in the eyes; it is more a feeling of tension or fatigue. Nevertheless, the eyes may ache considerably and be very tender to pressure, and according to V. Graefe, this occurs more frequently in muscular than in accommodative asthenopia.[3]

---

[1] Knapp's *Arch. of Oph.*, vol. xvii., p. 500.
[2] *Ibid.*, p. 508.
[3] Graefe's *Arch. f. Oph.*, bd. viii., 2, p. 324.

Ocular pain, the result of strain, may be limited to one eye. It is not at all uncommon to find that when *one* eye is astigmatic, but takes its share in the ocular work, that it *alone* becomes painful after use; and this is more especially the case when the astigmatism is of low degree.

Neuralgia.—Supra-orbital neuralgia, or "brow ague" is superficial pain in the region of distribution of the first division of the fifth nerve. It is often the result of eye-strain, especially in neuropathic subjects. It is probably purely reflex, and is analogous to the intense pain in the brow experienced by some people on eating ices.

III. OCULAR HEADACHE: Position.—The *position* and character of the headache vary. It may simply amount to a slight aching over the eyes, or at the back of the orbit; it may be a frontal headache. Sometimes it originates, and remains limited, as a vertical or occipital headache, or the pain may originate in the brows and pass to the vertex and occiput, and even down the spine. It may be unilateral, a typical hemicrania, and may be indistinguishable from a true megrim attack. Most writers (with the exception of V. Graefe[1]) agree that in ciliary asthenopia, the pain is generally orbital and frontal, and in muscular asthenopia, occipital and spinal. Culver suggests that temporal headache is due to astigmatism.[2]

Hewetson relates the case of a lady who suffered severely with pain at the back of the neck and tenderness of the spine. She was astigmatic, and was completely cured by glasses.[3]

Noyes says that the headache, on first waking in the

---

[1] *Vide supra.*
[2] *American Journal of Oph.*, vol. vi., p. 294.
[3] "General Neuroses having an Ophthalmic Origin," B.M.A. Meeting, 1888.

morning and increasing during the day, is the form generally present in muscular asthenopia.[1]

Landolt says: "A sensation of heaviness, which may pass into real pain, invades the eyes and forehead. This cephalalgia may take on the form of a genuine migraine, and render impossible not only all work, but even the fixation of the most distant objects."[2] Again, he mentions as phenomena of asthenopia: "At the bottom of the orbit, or even in the entire forehead, a sensation of pressure, which may become a genuine cephalalgia. The pain becomes more and more intense, and more and more frequent, sometimes even constant, and often takes on the character of a neuralgia."[3]

Hartridge says: "Headache is often a prominent symptom of asthenopia; it may take the form of heaviness or pain over the brow (which may or may not be combined with general headache); it is often periodic in character, and is always made worse by reading; frequently there is a tender spot on the top of the head, or pain in the occipital region, occasionally also there is pain in the back of the neck."[4]

It is impossible to lay down any rule as to the position of ocular headache; *the position varies with the individual.* Some people, when they have a headache, whatever the cause may be, describe it as frontal, others as vertical, and so on. The character also varies with the individual. In some people headache is generally superficial, akin to a neuralgia; others feel it as deep seated. It may be a dull, heavy ache, difficult to localise accurately, or

---

[1] *American Journal of Oph.*, vol. vii., p. 257.
[2] "Refraction and Accommodation," p. 370.
[3] *Ibid.*, p. 456.
[4] "Errors of Refraction and Accommodation," 1891, p. 557.

it may be a sharp shooting lancinating pain, that seems to start from some tender spot in the scalp or forehead. Some describe the pain as an opening and shutting of the skull, or as if a nail were being driven into the vertex. The commonest form of asthenopic headache is a dull pain over one or both brows.

It is important to remember that the headache of eye-strain is very often *periodic*. It does not follow that when the headache occurs it necessarily implies the presence of greater eye fatigue; the amount of strain may be the same as when no headache occurred, but the *individual* is in a different condition. Some other exhausting element may be present, such as worry, or the catamenial flow. It is a common thing to find ladies suffering from headache during or at the end of the menstrual period, and cause and effect are naturally linked together in the patient's mind, but the real cause may be eyestrain. The following is a case from my private note-book that will illustrate this:—

Mrs. V. O., age 31. Has four children. She has complained for years of periodical headaches; they appear about once a month and last sometimes a whole week, and are so severe during part of the time that she is obliged to keep her bed. She is slightly anæmic, but otherwise perfectly healthy. She has been thoroughly examined by a competent gynæcologist, who found no uterine or ovarian trouble. The catamenia are fairly regular, and the headache generally follows a period. Innumerable remedies have been tried, without avail.

Examination of the eyes without atropine revealed no defect, but under atropine the left eye was shown to be myopic in one meridian (oblique) to the extent of 1.5 D. The right eye was emmetropic. The astigmatism was fully corrected, and glasses were given to wear constantly, with the satisfactory result that her periodical headaches disappeared. Some time afterwards, thinking that she could discard her glasses she did so, with the result that the old headaches returned with all their severity, disappearing again on resuming the *constant* use of the glasses.

Here, then, was eyestrain, the result of astigmatism and anisometropia, which was only just sufficient to produce megrim when the nervous system was "below par."

Frequency of Ocular Headache.—Stevens reported that in one hundred consecutive cases of chronic headache in which the eyes were examined, he cured sixty-one by correcting the ocular defects.[1]

Gould says that out of 1,500 cases in private practice he found 75 per cent. of all headaches, and 95 per cent. of sick headache, were due to eyestrain.[2]

Culver gives a detailed account of nineteen cases where headache was the most prominent symptom, and was relieved by treating the ocular defect. In one of them, a girl aged 13 years, the intense headaches were accompanied by actual vomiting.[3]

Marlow says that heterophoria is more certain to produce headache than ametropia. Out of a total of 215 cases examined, 160 had *headache* (*i.e.*, 74.4 per cent.), and out of these only twenty-eight had orthophoria, and only in one, were emmetropia and orthophoria both present. He found that astigmatism of all kinds with simple hyperphoria was the most potent in producing headache, and myopia with esophoria the least.[4]

Ellis, of California, in 200 cases of errors of refraction, found 46.5 per cent. suffering from *headache*, and of these 29 per cent. complained of frontal, brow, or temporal headache; 21 per cent. general headache; 13 per cent. neuralgic headache; and 12 per cent. sick headache.[5]

---

[1] "Functional Nervous Diseases," 1887, p. 48.
[2] *Oph. Rev.*, vol. x., p. 280.
[3] *American Journal of Ophthalmology*, vol. vi., p. 192 and 296.
[4] *Oph. Rev.*, vol. viii., p. 353.
[5] *New York Med. Jour.*, April 30, 1892.

Bickerton, of Liverpool, says that out of 1,000 cases of refraction he found 277 suffering from headaches.[1] This gives a percentage of 27.7. From my own case book I find that of the patients who suffered from some error of refraction or mal-adjustment of the eyes, about 30 per cent. complained of headache. Therefore we may assert that in England between one-fourth and one-third of patients suffering from refractive or other error of their eyes suffer from headache.

Ætiology and Pathology.—Liveing says that the immediate antecedent of an attack of megrim, a "nerve storm," is a condition of unstable equilibrium and gradually accumulating tension in the parts of the nervous system more immediately concerned, while the paroxysm itself may be likened to a *storm*, by which this condition is dispersed and equilibrium for the time restored.[2] It is thus very possible that eyestrain may be just the impetus required to start one of the attacks—in other words, among the different exciting causes in different cases of megrim, eyestrain may rank as one. Most writers agree that the age for megrim is between puberty and thirty, which is the period during which asthenopia is very common. But there is no doubt that many cases that have been considered as true megrim were nothing more than cases of asthenopia. Liveing points out[3] that Piorry first drew attention to the ophthalmic theory of migraine. He thought the attack was due in some cases to prolonged straining of the eyes on small objects or with bad illumination; that the morbid action was in the retina and iris, spreading to the fifth pair of nerves causing pain, and to the eighth pair and great sympathetic causing

---

[1] *Lancet*, 1887, vol. ii., p. 303.
[2] "Megrim and Sick Headaches," 1873, p. 336.
[3] *Ibid.*, p. 257.

nausea, &c. At the same time he considered the stomach to be the primary cause.

Martin considers that ophthalmic megrim is due to astigmatism. He says: "Toute migraine pour manifester exige trois facteurs—l'élément constitutionel de nature diathesique, la contraction partielle" (du muscle ciliaire) "et une cause occasionelle variable selon les cas;"[1] and he cites a number of cases showing the connection between the two; the attacks of migraine being very much lessened by the correction of the astigmatism.

Haig says that migraine, or megrim, bilious or sick headache, is nothing more than what he calls "uric acid headache"—a headache due to the excess of uric acid in the blood (Uric-acidæmia).[2] In a person, then, with conditions for a uric-acid headache, eyestrain, although not the primary cause, takes its place among the various peripheral irritations that may start the attack.

Lauder Brunton says: "It would be going too far to say that frontal headache is always due to an abnormal condition of the eyes, but I believe it is so much more frequently than we would at all suspect. Even the frontal headache which occurs in derangement of the stomach and biliousness is, I think, very frequently connected with an abnormal condition of the eyes to which the indigestion gives rise; for if we press the fingers upon the eyeballs during a bilious headache, we not unfrequently find that they are abnormally tense, and the intra-ocular pressure high, so that the eyeball feels almost like a marble under the finger." And again he says: "But frontal headache is not the only one which may arise from abnormal conditions of the eyes, for megrim or sick headache is very

---

[1] *Annales d'Oculisque*, 1888, i. p. 123.
[2] "Uric Acid," 1892, p. 71.

frequently associated with, and probably dependent on, inequality of the eyes, either in the way of astigmatism, myopia, or hypermetropia."[1]

Liveing says that the "nerve storms" in megrim have their point of departure or principal focus in the optic thalami, and that the normal course is from above downwards (to the nuclei of the vagus), and from before backwards in the sensory tract.[2] This explains the peculiar visual phenomena such as "teichopsia," &c., and other symptoms of "ophthalmic megrim" when the ocular trouble is the *effect;* but when it is the *cause* the "point of departure" must be in the eyes themselves or their connections, and the headaches must be brought about somewhat as follows. The ciliary muscle, or the external muscles of the eye, or both, are being overtaxed, hence an excessive supply of blood is passing to them leading to active, and, if kept up, to passive, congestion. This congestion will not be limited to the muscles in question, but in time will pass to other parts of the eye, leading to watery red eyes, or in other words, to chronic conjunctivitis. This congestion will either cause, or make the muscles prone to, pain, and added to the pain of fatigue, will account for the feeling of tension or pain in the eyes themselves; and the intimate connection of the nerves supplying these muscles with the fifth pair will cause the morbid action to spread to these latter nerves, and explain the frontal headache. Through the connection of the fifth nerve with the sympathetic, we can understand how this morbid action can travel to the dura mater, pia mater and sensory layer of the cortex of the brain; and this action

---

[1] "On the Pathology and Treatment of some Forms of Headache," *St. Bartholomew's Hospital Reports*, vol. xix., p. 336.

[2] *Op. cit.*, p. 396.

will be helped in most cases by the presence of cerebral hyperæmia or passive congestion, due in some cases to the position of the head (as bending or stooping over the work), and in all cases by increased blood supply to the head caused by the special use of the brain at the time, or produced by the same stimulus that takes the increased blood supply to the eyes.

Lippencott's cases, in which there was a sharply defined redness resembling episcleritis over the insertion of the internal recti tendons, associated with "insufficiency" those muscles, indicate an excessive hypera muscles produced by over-exertion. Jackson s this condition is the same as that produced in the muscles of a base-ball pitcher's arm when it fails from over-use.[1]

This seems to be the most probable theory of the mechanism by which ocular headache is produced. We really know very little about the actual seat of the pain in headaches. When the pain is quite local and superficial, as for instance in some brow aches, it is more of a neuralgia than a headache; but even in such cases, as also in the more diffuse superficial headaches, the origin of the pain may really be in the higher centres of the brain through which the superficial pain is perceived, as Gowers has pointed out.[2] In deeper-seated headaches, whether the pain is in the cerebral substance itself, or what is more probable, in the membranes, we cannot say. There is no doubt that cerebral congestion by increasing the intra-cranial pressure, may cause, or tend to cause, pain. Gowers says: " If the sensory cells of the cortex, in which the cranial and intra-cranial sensitive structures are represented, are the most readily influenced of all the sensory cells, we

---

[1] *Trans. of the American Oph. Society*, vol. iv., p. 482.
[2] "Nervous System," vol. ii., p. 795.

can understand that headache should result from vascular repletion."[1] Everyone knows from experience the increased severity of a headache caused by the stooping position.

Sometimes the headache in eyestrain is purely *reflex*.

Lauder Brunton says, in writing of the headache caused by carious teeth, "The mechanism of the headache here is that the irritation in a tooth, for example, acting through the vaso-motor nerves, causes vascular spasm, and this vascular spasm causes the pain of headache."[2] In the same way, the eyestrain may through the sympathetic also produce the same effect.

Hewetson says sick-headaches "occur in neurotic subjects, the sympathetic system of whose brain is irritated by the eye attempting to overcome its defect; this irritation and pain apparently depresses the individual, and reflects its influence to the heart and stomach by the pneumogastric nerve."[3]

IV. **Vertigo and Sickness.**—Diplopia is the chief cause of these symptoms, and consequently it is mostly found in muscular asthenopia. If the internal recti are subjected to excessive strain, they will break down from stress of work, and will relax suddenly or gradually, and their opponents, the external recti, that have been in a passive state of tension, actively contract and pull over the eyes causing diplopia.

Schiötz,[4] of Christiania, writing of the symptoms of muscular asthenopia, says, "We rarely hear complaints of

---

[1] *Op. cit.*, p. 797.   [2] *Op. cit.*, p. 333.
[3] "The Relation between Sick-headaches and defective Sight chiefly resulting from Astigmatism: their pathology and treatment by glasses." *Medical Times and Gazette*, 1885, vol. i., p. 375.
[4] *Knapp's Arch. of Oph.*, vol. xix., p. 176.

objects becoming indistinct, wavering, or double." This is certainly not my experience. Patients suffering from muscular asthenopia very often *volunteer* the remark that they "*see double.*" Very often this diplopia is only temporary, for the very good reason that the cause is removed by the patient. In convergence "insufficiency," if the work is too near, the effort of the internal recti to preserve binocular vision is so great that the muscles refuse to work at such high pressure any longer; the result is diplopia, with the inevitable necessity on the part of the patient to suspend work. Sometimes the lesser symptoms, viz., pain and headache, cause the patient to cease work before diplopia arises.

Alfred Graefe, writing in 1880, says : " Die betreffenden Individuen koennen sich nur kuerzere Zeit mit nahe liegenden Objecten (Lesen, Schreiben, etc.) ohne Gêne beschaeftigen, dann erscheinen dieselben plötzlich *doppelt*, Zeilen und Buchstaben laufen wirr in einander, waehrend gleichzeitig ein Gefuehl des unbehagens oder schmertzhaften Zwanges auf beiden oder vorzugsweise auf einem Auge lastet."[1]

The double vision causes a "retinal confusion ;" this confusion produces on the individual a sense of want of equilibrium, causing vertigo and, if prolonged, sickness, vomiting, dyspepsia, palpitation and dyspnœa. Everyone is familiar with the giddiness produced by gazing at a pronounced "check" pattern, or looking through a stereoscope or glasses that do not suit the sight; and many people are unable to travel during the day with their backs to the engine on account of the feeling of sickness that is induced.[2] In both cases it is the "unfamiliar retinal confusion" that causes the trouble.

---

[1] *Graefe Saemisch Hdbh.*, bd. vi., p. 192.   [2] See p. 39.

Persons who cannot travel during the day with their backs to the engine or horses can do so with impunity at night, and hence the cause must be connected with the passage of objects seen from the carriage window. Our forward mode of progression familiarises us with the passage of objects *towards* us, but we are unfamiliar with the reverse, and this may be the cause of the symptoms. Again, the vertigo experienced by most people on looking down from a great height is probably another instance of this "unfamiliarity." Looking upwards for a great distance produces no such effect, because we are perfectly familiar with the practice; and sailors and others who are accustomed to "dizzy" heights can generally look down with impunity, because the "unfamiliarity" has become familiar. Priestley Smith has suggested that the presence of latent deviation of the eyes may account for the giddiness, for the movements of the eyes downwards are usually associated with convergence, and the necessity for parallel vision may produce diplopia or a tendency to it. Brewer, in a paper on "Apparent Movement of Objects associated with giddiness,"[1] refers to the giddiness produced by the eye trying to fix moving objects, as out of a railway carriage window. He says that if the eyes are not allowed to follow the moving objects then there is no giddiness, and if the image falls on the side of the retina there is no giddiness. He considers the giddiness is due to secondary apparent after-movements, and is an optical, and not a muscular, impression. Bain, on the other hand, considers that vertigo is always a *motor* symptom. Ross says diplopia causes the patient to become "*confused* on endeavouring to grasp objects. This constant confusion

---

[1] *Trans. Oph. Soc.*, vol. ix., p. 176.

causes great fatigue, vertigo, and sometimes vomiting."[1] And he says, "vertigo appears to be the subjective correlation of want of co-ordination between the various muscular contractions necessary for adjusting the body to the different objects which surround it in space. . . . Vertigo is usually accompanied by motor phenomena in the region of distribution of the pneumogastric, such as feeble and irregular pulse, irregular respiration and vomiting."[2]

The probability is that vertigo in all cases is a *motor phenomenon*, and that although in many cases of ocular vertigo, the symptoms appear to be caused by "retinal confusion," this very confusion causes a sense of instability. In diplopia the non-correspondence of the retinal images and the false projection, produce first a "confusion," and this confusion produces a sense of "want of equilibrium." Gowers says, "There is an error in the unconscious inference of the relation of the body to seen objects, and this element in the impressions that influence the equilibrial centre is at variance with others, and either the *discord* or the disturbance of the centre is felt as giddiness."[3]

The mechanism of vertigo is even more difficult to theorise upon, than headache. Physiologists agree that the cerebellum is the "seat of equilibrium," and that organic or functional disturbance of this centre produces vertigo. By what path the "contradictory sensory impressions" find their way to the cerebellum is uncertain. The feeling of sickness, vomiting, dyspepsia and palpitation so often associated with vertigo are explained by the connection of the pneumogastric with the cerebellum. Gowers says, "It is probable that the gastric fibres of the

---

[1] "Nervous System," 1883, vol. i., p. 436.
[2] *Ibid*, vol. i., p. 92.   [3] *Op. cit.*, vol. ii., p. 724.

vagus have a connection with the middle lobe of the cerebellum." [1]

Insomnia.—In a paper on "General Neuroses having an Ophthalmic Origin," [2] Hewetson, of Leeds, says, "This particular symptom I observed in many cases the subjects of astigmatism," and he mentions a case of a University man suffering from insomnia; he was astigmatic, and after the error was corrected the insomnia disappeared, although he was doing the same amount of reading.

Ranney [3] and Ellis [4] also cite numerous cases of sleeplessness cured by relieving the refractive or muscular defect of the eyes.

Insomnia is a complaint that may not be volunteered, but that can be elicited from many patients who are the subjects of severe asthenopia. The hyperæmia of the brain, the headaches, and the general low tone of the nervous system easily explain the phenomenon.

Eyestrain tends to produce or increase myopia.—One effect of unrelieved eyestrain is to produce increased intraocular pressure through the congestion of the vessels, and consequent myopia. In a paper on "Some Remarks on Asthenopia and Changes of Refraction," [5] Norris has drawn attention to this and cited cases.

V. **The Relation between Eyestrain and Severe Neuroses.**—At the present day, the universal recognition of asthenopia as the cause of many troubles, that formerly were not supposed to be in any way connected with it,

---

[1] *Op. cit.*, vol. ii., p. 724.
[2] Section of Ophthal., Brit. Med. Assoc. Meeting, 1888.
[3] *New York Med. Journ.*, June 11, 1892.
[4] *Ibid*, April 30, 1892.
[5] *Trans. of the American Ophth. Soc.*, vol. iv., p. 369.

has led, as one might expect, to the "pendulum swinging" too much the other way. There is a tendency to assign asthenopia as the cause of numerous diseases that it can possibly be only the effect of, if even there is any connection. For instance, it has been claimed that eye-strain will cause *anæmia* or *constipation*, and that the correction of as small an error of refraction as half a dioptre, or even less, will remove these complaints!

Stevens, of New York, says, "Difficulties attending the functions of accommodating and of adjusting the eyes in the act of vision, or irritations arising from the nerves involved in these processes, are among the most prolific sources of nervous disturbances, and more frequently than other conditions constitute a neuropathic tendency."[1] His conclusions are based upon observations in 2692 cases of nervous diseases. He maintains that by correcting the ocular defect he has cured the disease in a large proportion of the cases. He includes in his list of cures, headache (83.6 per cent. cured), migraine, neuralgia (83.53 per cent. cured), spinal irritation and neurasthenia, chorea, epilepsy and mental disorders. He says that out of 118 cases of chorea in children examined by him, no less than 113 had some refractive defect, 78 suffering from simple hyperopia.[2] A commission was appointed by the New York Neurological Society in 1889 to report on the treatment of epilepsy and chorea by the correction of ocular defects, and the answer was that Stevens had not proved his case.[3]

Ranney asserts that he has cured or relieved epilepsy, neurasthenia, neuralgia, chorea, hystero-epilepsy, melan-

---

[1] "Functional Nervous Diseases," 1887, p. 21.
[2] *Op. cit.*, p. 91.
[3] *Oph. Rev.*, vol. ix., p. 83.

cholia and other nervous diseases by correcting the ocular defect, and so removing the eyestrain.[1]

Colburn[2] relates the case of a man, aged 24, who had been unsuccessfully treated for "petit mal." He had manifest $H = .5$ D. and latent $H = +2$ D. and insufficiency of the external recti. The latter was overcome by exercise with prisms, and $+ 2$ D. glasses were ordered for constant use, with the result that the epilepsy was cured.

At the June meeting of the American Medical Association, 1887, Frothingham and others reported cases of epilepsy cured by the relief of eyestrain. Frothingham's case was a woman, aged 24, who had suffered from epilepsy since the age of 11. She was found to have hyperopia of 2 D., and glasses of $+ 1.5$ D. were given her to wear constantly, with the result that the seizures were entirely checked, the cure having lasted two years.[3]

Fulton reports three cases of chorea in children, confined to the muscles of the lids and face, caused by strain of the external muscles of the eye, in which correction of the refractive trouble, with tenotomy of one or other of the recti completely relieved the sufferers.[4] Gould has reported under the heading of "Reflex Neuroses due to Eyestrain" one case of chorea of several years' duration, one case of dyspepsia (!) of twenty years' standing, cured, and a case of cardiac palpitation relieved by glasses.[5]

On the other hand, Allen Starr, in a paper on "The Relation between Peripheral Irritation and Nervous Phe-

---

[1] *Knapp, Arch. of Oph.*, vol. xvii., p. 105, and *New York Med. Journal*, June 11 and 18, 1892.
[2] *Knapp, Arch. of Oph.*, vol. xviii., p. 118.
[3] *Oph. Rev.*, vol. vi., p. 245.
[4] *American Journal of Oph.*, vol. vii., p. 26.
[5] *Knapp, Arch. of Oph.*, vol. xix., p. 107.

nomena, with Special Reference to Eyestrain,"[1] ridicules the idea that eyestrain can produce neuroses such as epilepsy and chorea, and he says that while eyestrain may be a source of nervous manifestation, it was a rare cause of nervous disease, and he classes it with other peripheral irritations.

Many writers have observed that epilepsy may be relieved, and slight cases cured, by an operation. Pechdo relates a case where epilepsy was cured by the enucleation of an eye,[2] and it has been suggested that those cases of epilepsy that have been cured by tenotomy of one of the eye muscles, owe this cure to the *shock* of the operation. It is not at all uncommon to come across children suffering from slight chorea, cured by glasses. The following is a good example, from my case-book :—

D. L., age 8, a well nourished healthy-looking boy, suffers from most incessant blinking associated with choreiform movements of the facial muscles. He has also slight chronic conjunctivitis.

$$V = \begin{cases} R = \frac{6}{36} \\ L = \frac{6}{24} \end{cases} \text{ latent convergence for distance} = \frac{1}{6} \text{ m. a.}$$

Under atropine the examination shows compound myopic astigmatism, and the following glasses were ordered :—

R.			L.
	30°	10°	
− 1 D sph.	\	/	− 1 D sph.
− 1 D cyl.	\	/	− 2 D cyl.

The glasses gave him $V = \frac{6}{9}$ c̄ B. E., and were ordered for constant use.

He returned six months later a different boy. The eyes were normal in appearance and $V = \begin{cases} R \frac{6}{6} \\ L \frac{6}{9} \end{cases}$, the chorea had disappeared, and the blinking was only very occasional.

It is not very difficult to find a real explanation for these cures when they take place. There is no doubt that up

---

[1] *Medical Record*, Jan. 4, 1890.
[2] *Rec. d'Oph.*, 1887, p. 346.

to the present we have no proof that such diseases as epilepsy and chorea owe their existence to eyestrain, but eyestrain, like any other peripheral irritation, such as indigestion, &c., may start an attack in an epileptic or choreic patient; and if the eyestrain is removed the peripheral irritation is likewise removed, and the attacks are more likely to be fewer or milder, or even disappear altogether.

VI. RELATIVE FREQUENCY OF ASTHENOPIA.—

Eyestrain is chiefly caused by some abnormal condition of the eyes. What is the proportion of normal vision to abnormal vision?

Jackson, of Philadelphia, in a paper on "The Absolute Static Refraction of the Eye,"[1] reports that out of 4,000 eyes examined during complete paralysis of accommodation, only 51, *i.e.*, 1.3 per cent., were normal.

Randall reports an examination of the eyes of 142 medical students. He found only 16 really emmetropic without the use of a mydriatic, which would probably have considerably reduced even this low average.[2] Again, in a paper criticising the various statistics on record, based on the examination of the refraction in large schools, &c., numbering 115 separate investigations, and including 146,522 examinations, he says, "Emmetropia, in a mathematically strict sense, has probably no existence. Approximate emmetropia (Ametropia $< \pm .5$ D) is infrequent in all ages, probably at no epoch exceeding 10 per cent."[3]

Out of a school of 150 children of the average age of eight years, lately examined by me, I only found *one*

---

[1] *Trans. of the American Oph. Soc.*, vol. v., p. 435.
[2] *American Journal of Oph.*, vol. viii., p. 40.
[3] *American Journal of the Med. Sciences*, July, 1885.

child with perfectly normal vision in *both* eyes, and 41 with normal vision in one eye—that is, less than one-third had fairly good sight. Unfortunately it was found impossible to examine all the eyes under a mydriatic, but 25 of the worst cases were so examined and proved to be all cases of hyperopia or hyperopic astigmatism.

The hyperopic or flat eye is the undeveloped eye, and most writers agree that the vision of young children is hyperopic. Horstmann, of Berlin, says that 88 per cent. of new-born children are hyperopic, and 86 per cent. between the ages of four and six. The majority of these hyperopic eyes are intended by nature to become emmetropic, but in a large number of cases instead of this happening, as development proceeds they "overshoot the mark" and become myopic, or astigmatism may develop, and this is the result of civilisation! Roosa says that only a very small proportion of adults, say 7 per cent., have absolutely emmetropic eyes.[1] From his private case book, out of a total of 6,455 patients he found 1,445 suffered from asthenopia, all of them having some abnormal condition of the eyes. Again he says, " Not only all the world have faulty refraction, but very few people possess equilibrium of the ocular muscles," and out of 103 persons examined who complained of *no* trouble with their eyes—who read, wrote and sewed without headaches or any other symptom of strain—only 17, *i.e.*, 16 per cent., had muscular equilibrium.

There is then no doubt that the perfectly normal eye is the *exception*. How is it then that asthenopia, common as it is, is not universal? The fact is, as Brudenell Carter[2] has pointed out, the liability to asthenopia of any nation bears a distinct relation to the neurotic condition of the

---

[1] *Trans. American Oph. Soc.*, 1878.
[2] Hunterian Lectures, 1877.

people. The nervo-muscular excitability of the Americans explains the enormous preponderance of asthenopia in the United States (see fig. 1, p. 28). Thus we should expect to find that people with an unstable nervous system, who are emotional and easily excitable, prone to suffer from asthenopia if the conditions for it exist, whereas other individuals in a healthy mental and physical state, although perhaps suffering from a greater tendency to asthenopia, are yet able to ward it off. Again, the condition of life is an important factor; Burnett says, " Like nervous prostration, I think the asthenopia and headaches of heterophoria and ametropia is a disease developed largely by the American method of living."[1] The individual who lives at high pressure, as our cousins over the Atlantic do, is a very likely subject for asthenopia. In these days of telephones and cables, when our business men do as much work in a day as our forefathers did in a week, we find an explanation of the increase of asthenopia with increase of civilisation.

We then see that the symptoms of eyestrain are *nervous* phenomena, naturally most prone to make their appearance in a *nervous* age or in *nervous* people, and dependent upon either an abnormal use of, or an abnormal condition of the eyes.

In a very interesting article on "Eyesight in Schools,"[2] Brudenell Carter published the results of the Philadelphia committee, who examined carefully the eyes of 2,596 children. Some very interesting statistics were obtained, showing the relation of asthenopia to the refraction of the eye.

Perusal of the following table (fig. 1) will show that the

---

[1] *Trans. Am. Oph. Soc.*, vol. vi., part 1, p. 221.
[2] Pamphlet reprinted from *Medical Times and Gazette* April 22 and May 2, 1885.

percentage of asthenopia in emmetropia was 21 per cent., and that this steadily rose to 72 per cent. in myopic astigmatism, and 74 per cent. in mixed astigmatism.

I have in fig. 2 made a table showing the relation of asthenopia to the refraction, from my own cases. I have taken these from my *private* case-book, because the notes

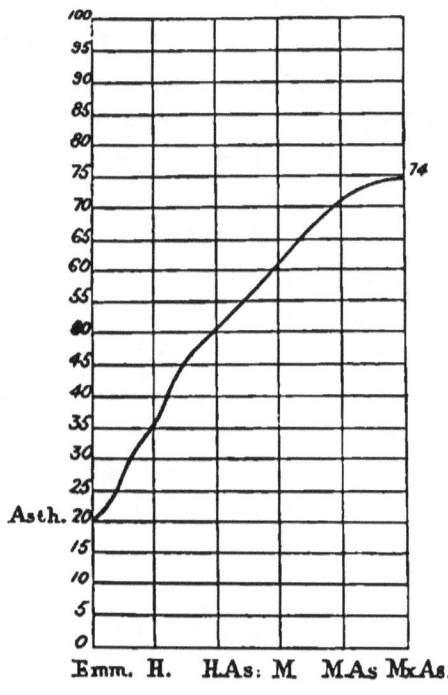

Fig. 1.

were fuller and the examination more complete. Out of 317 cases 105 suffered from asthenopia, that is, *one-third*.

Comparison of the American table with mine reveals some important differences. I only show 2 per cent. of emmetropic asthenopia, whereas fig. 1 shows 21 per cent. At first I thought that my low percentage was due to the fact that the patients being of the wealthier classes, there was a natural absence of engravers, seamstresses, &c., but on consulting my hospital record, I find that out of 1,995 patients who consulted me because of some error of refraction or symptom of asthenopia, only 52, *i.e.*, 2.6 per cent., suffered from emmetropic asthenopia. Our

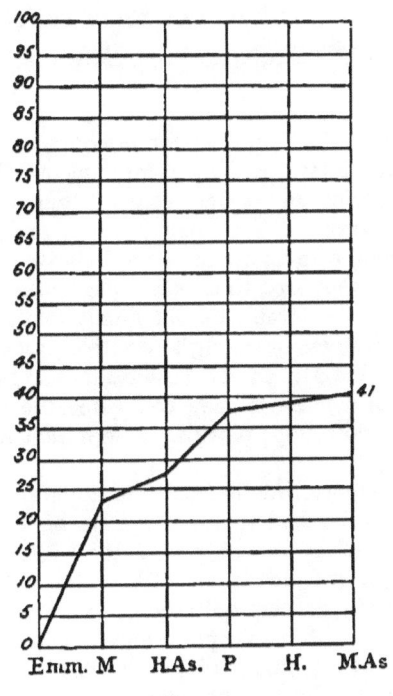

FIG. 2.

averages of hyperopic asthenopia are not so different, mine being 39 per cent. and the American 35 per cent.; but whereas in the latter table hyperopia stands lowest of all the errors that occasion asthenopia, in my experience it stands highest but one. I have introduced presbyopia, which is absent in fig. 1. In 77 cases asthenopia was present in 30, *i.e.*, almost 39 per cent. My highest average was 41 per cent. of asthenopia in myopic astigmatism, whereas in the American table this reached 72 per cent.; and the highest reached was 74 per cent. in mixed astigmatism, in which I find only 4 cases recorded and no history of asthenopia.

VII. DIFFERENTIAL DIAGNOSIS OF ASTHENOPIA.—Mistakes have often been made in assigning as the cause of the symptoms of asthenopia some serious disease, such as brain mischief. The case that Brudenell Carter relates is a good example :—

A young man at Oxford, reading for honours, complained that his work was constantly interrupted by symptoms which compelled him to seek medical advice, and which were attributed to brain disease. Under advice he gave up work, left Oxford, and after consulting various medical men, who all concurred in believing him the victim of brain disease, he was ordered to take a voyage to Australia and back. This he did, with no result, and he was finally told to give up all idea of going into any business or taking any active part in life.

The father consulted Mr. Carter, because he had heard that oculists used an instrument wherewith they could see the circulation in the brain, and in the forlorn hope that the examination might throw some light on the case.

The patient's memory, intelligence and mental faculties were all unimpaired. Before he had read a page he became the subject of double vision, followed by vertigo, and, if the effort was continued, by sickness, palpitation and headache. When he had not been trying to read he was in all respects quite well. Examination showed the patient to be myopic, with his far point only 8 inches from the cornea. He had *binocular* vision, and had never worn spectacles, but with concaves of 8-inch focal length, distant vision was nearly normal.

He was given 8-inch concaves for distance and 14-inch concaves for reading, with the special command that the work was never to be brought nearer than eighteen inches, with the result that he was cured.[1]

Brudenell Carter says: " I think it follows that in any case of pain or distress about the head, the nature of which is not fully apparent, it will be a prudent precaution to

---

[1] *Clinical Transactions*, vol. viii., p. 13.

examine into the state of vision and of refraction, and into the strength of the recti muscles and into the conditions under which they are called upon to act."

Day says: "When attacks of vomiting and headache come on in young persons who strain their eyes, the symptoms, in some of these cases, are thought to be due to brain disease, whereas they are really owing to defects of vision, or errors of refraction, which result in myopia, hypermetropia or astigmatism."[1]

Hence it is most important to thoroughly test the eyes of all who complain of headaches or any other asthenopic symptom, and if this were done at first instead of last, as is so often the case, a large amount of disappointment to the medical man and the patient would be avoided in many cases. It is important to remember that the headache of brain tumours is independent of any visual effort, and that optic neuritis is to be looked out for as a very probable association. Frontal or temporal pain, which may be more of the character of a neuralgia, is often caused by a decayed tooth. It is possible that eyestrain may also exist, and we then have the two reflex causes acting together, the one increasing the effect of the other. Hence in all cases where correction of the ocular defect does not yield a satisfactory result, we should have the teeth overhauled by an experienced dentist.

The diagnosis of the particular variety of asthenopia is only made by a thorough examination of the refraction and muscular equilibrium of the eyes. V. Graefe has suggested the following points as a help in diagnosing convergence from ciliary strain:—

(1) The symptoms of muscular asthenopia last longer

---

[1] "Headaches," 1888, by W. H. Day, M.D., p. 215.

and require a longer rest for their removal than those of accommodative asthenopia.

(2) The haziness (verschwimmen) is more a "running together and through one another" of the letters than an indistinctness of outline, and this passes on sometimes to definite double vision. Further, he says that when this happens many patients actually feel "that one eye is turning out."

(3) A large number of patients find relief in covering up one eye; and

(4) In putting the object further back.

(5) The sensitive troubles are more localised in the eyes themselves and the region of the brow, rather than in the form of headaches.[1]

---

[1] *Graefe, Arch. f. Oph.*, bd. 8, ii., p. 323.

PART II.

CILIARY STRAIN (ACCOMMODATIVE ASTHENOPIA.)

CILIARY STRAIN (ACCOMMODATIVE ASTHENOPIA.)

I. THE CAUSES OF CILIARY STRAIN.—Fatigue of the ciliary muscle occurs in :—

EMMETROPIA *Direct*
  { i. Abuse in the healthy.
  { ii. Diminished accommodative power, due to
      (*a*) Age.
      (*b*) Nervo-muscular debility ["Neurasthenic Asthenopia"].
      (*c*) Congenital defect.
      [(*d*) Disease of the eye.]
Reflex ("Reflex Asthenopia").
AMETROPIA ("Accommodative Asthenopia") in :—
    1. Hyperopia.
    2. Astigmatism.
    3. Presbyopia.
    4. Anisometropia.

II. CILIARY STRAIN IN EMMETROPIA (strain of the accommodation in those who have no error of refraction) :—

In the perfectly healthy.—This is simple ordinary fatigue, and is Nature's outcry against the overuse or abuse of the ciliary muscle. Who has not, some time or another, after, say, an evening's close work, complained of the eyes, and often the head, aching? The night's rest removes these symptoms of eyestrain, as it does most other forms of fatigue. Two men similarly constituted in every respect may each read eight hours a day, and while one suffers from asthenopia towards the end of the day, the other may escape it by giving his ciliary muscle frequent intervals of rest. It is the *continuous close work that induces the fatigue*. West, in speaking of the headache of children, says, "I have frequently found it dependant on *too* continuous application, though the number of hours devoted to study in the course of the day may not have been by any means excessive."[1] Faulty illumination is a very great help in producing the strain, hence it is the evening work that should be specially avoided by those liable to suffer. All artificial lighting is more or less defective. It is hardly necessary to mention that reading in a railway carriage, generally very badly illuminated, is very pernicious. Those who have to work for their living cannot, as a rule, pick and choose as to the time they should use their accommodative powers, hence we find compositors, newspaper readers, seamstresses, machinists, workers at fine art needlework, or embroidery, and gold lace workers, all suffer more or less from eyestrain. Jewellers, watchmakers, and precious stone workers, mostly use a magnifying-glass called a "watchmaker's glass," and thus save their ciliary muscle to some extent. The stooping position of the head that most close workers maintain causes congestion of the eyes, and renders them more liable to suffer from the strain.

It is a matter of common observation that children approach their eyes very closely to their work. This bad habit probably begins, through the little ones having to pore over the letters and words, when they are learning to read. Very often it is due to the faulty illumination of the schoolroom. Some time ago I was examining the eyesight of a class of girls, whose average age was eight years, in one of our London parish schools; with hardly an exception

---

[1] Lumleian Lectures, 1871.

they read at a distance of 10-12 cms., although most of them could see equally well to read at 33 cms.

On examining their class-room I found the cause of this. It was a long room with windows on one of the long walls; the forms were arranged along the other long wall, and the children faced these windows. The reason given me for this arrangement was, that the teacher being with her back to the light opposite the children, and the light falling full on them, she was thus able to see them and watch them much better, than if *she* had faced the light, and the children had taken her place. The effect on the children was, of course, that when they had to read in class, in order to prevent the dazzling effect of the light streaming into their eyes, the book had to be held up close to the face, or the head had to stoop to the book.

Children invariably hold their little heads close to the slate or paper when learning to write, and this bad position very often becomes a fixed habit.

Priestley Smith, in an article on "Means for the Prevention of Myopia," has written at some length on the subject, and has given some very good illustrations of the good and bad positions in reading and writing.[1]

Fuchs also refers to this matter in his book on "The Causes and Prevention of Blindness."[2]

This close application of the eyes to the work not only produces ciliary strain, but also strain of the convergent muscles (see Part III). Fortunately the young have such a large range of accommodation and convergence that they

---

[1] *Oph. Rev.*, vol. v., p. 153.
[2] *Oph. Rev.*, vol. iv., p. 93.

All those connected with the education of the young should read Priestley Smith's paper and Cohn's book on the "Hygiene of the Eye," especially the chapter on school desks.

escape asthenopia as a rule, if they are emmetropic, but the habit is a very bad one, and is liable to cause myopia.

In those whose accommodation power is diminished.

In *old age*, apart from the alteration in the refraction (presbyopia), there is a degeneration of the fibres of the ciliary muscle (Jessop).[1]

III. NEURASTHENIC ASTHENOPIA.—In those recovering from a long illness, the ciliary muscles suffer from impairment with the rest of the body. In pregnancy, and lactation, the insufficient supply of blood to the brain and eye produces the same effect (Power).[2] The general nervous prostration that so often follows an attack of epidemic "*Influenza*" very often causes decreased power in the ciliary muscle. I have lately seen a number of patients complaining of asthenopia for the first time in their lives, and who have dated the trouble back to an attack of this disease. Many of them were emmetropes who had thus become prematurely presbyopic.

We have already seen that highly-strung nervous people are specially prone to eyestrain, and there is a class called "neurasthenics" who, very specially, belong to this category.

Wilbrand says *neurasthenic asthenopia* is the local manifestation of a nervous affection, the special character of which is nervous instability, increased excitability, and the consequences—easily induced fatigue. Some of the leading symptoms of this disease are irritability, insomnia and hyperæsthesia of most of the senses, accompanied often by illusions, and mental delusions. Extreme sensitiveness of the whole system is very marked, and the eyes take part in

---

[1] *Oph. Rev.*, vol. vii., p. 226.
[2] *Trans. Oph. Soc.*, vol. viii., p. 35.

this in very many cases (more especially if any error of refraction is present).

Extreme susceptibility to "confusion" in vision is a well-marked symptom; thus people so affected cannot travel with their backs to the engine or horses, and he mentions a case of a highly neurasthenic gentleman, who could not look at anyone wearing clothes of a pronounced check pattern, without suffering from eyestrain, manifesting itself in headache and malaise.[1]

The eyes easily become inflamed, and ciliary spasm and blepharo-spasm often appear. The natural result of this hyper-sensitiveness is early fatigue, and ciliary strain is soon induced, and accompanying very often we find muscular and retinal asthenopia. After reading for a short time the words grow misty and disappear, and after a short rest the effects of the fatigue vanish, only to reappear when the accommodation is again used.

Under the heading of "Neurasthenia," MacFarlane says "the dimness of vision may depend upon errors of refraction which in health could be overcome by muscular effort, but which the exhaustion renders impossible."[2]

Weir Mitchell, referring to neurasthenics, says "fatigue of vision for near work is a common condition," and "is apt to persist long after all other troubles have vanished."[3]

W. J. Collins considers the failure of accommodation in neurasthenics is due to an actual cycloparesis. He says: "The failure of accommodative power after diphtheria, in the puerperal state, or in association with miscarriage or disturbed menstruation, and also that to which I desire to draw particular attention—the asthenopia of neurasthenics—

---

[1] *Oph. Rev.*, vol. iii., p. 10.
[2] "Insomnia," by A. W. MacFarlane, M.D., p. 105.
[3] "Fat and Blood and how to make Them," 1877, p. 86.

I take to belong to the same category. In all there is a faulty blood metabolism, and consequent neuro-muscular debility, and it would seem that unstriped muscle suffers seriously from such defective hæmopoiesis, the heart and arterial muscles exhibit lack of tone, the pulse is soft, often irregular, and palpitation is common, the muscular fibre of the intestines suffers, and chronic constipation is a frequent concomitant ; the ciliary muscle, with or without associated affection of the iris, is similarly weakened, and the amplitude of accommodation is seriously restricted."[1]

The prognosis of neurasthenic asthenopia is neither good nor bad. The visual symptoms rarely develop into actual disease, but although they may be relieved or cured for a time, the general nervous excitability scarcely ever quite disappears, and so relapses are common ; although I have seen several cases I have never yet seen a complete cure.

IV. Anæmia is another disease that is a common cause of ciliary strain. Here again we have faulty blood metabolism ; and the lack of sufficient oxygen-giving blood naturally induces diminished vital power. Anæmia shows itself in young girls, very often at the age of 14 or 15, and this is just the period when more work is forced upon the ciliary muscles. It is the time in their school life when hard work either begins or reaches its maximum, they are beginning to prepare for those severe tests—examinations. Thus, instead of diminished ciliary power they want more. The headaches so often accompanying anæmia are often induced and if not induced, exaggerated by eyestrain.

Giraud Teulon found among 727 cases of ciliary strain in school children with Hyperopia, 532 *i.e.*, 63 per cent. suffering from anæmia and adynæmia.[2]

---

[1] R.L.O.H. Reports, vol. xii., p. 328.
[2] *Knapp's Archiv.*, vol. xv., p. 223.

Constipation, the fruitful source of so many ills may, unaided, be insufficient to cause eyestrain, but combined with some other cause may be "the last straw that breaks the camel's back." Chronic constipation causes portal congestion, and in time general congestion, in which the eyes partake, and we see every day evidences of it as a prime cause of general impairment of the health.

Parinaud refers to the "cephalalgia of adolescence" occurring between the ages of 15 and 18, and more frequent in males than females. He says the pain is frontal, sometimes localised as two painful points at the roots of the eyebrows. Use of the eyes always intensifies the pain.[1]

Congenital Deficiency of the Ciliary Muscle.—Many persons fall short of the accommodative power of the average emmetrope, and sometimes the only explanation is, that the ciliary muscle is abnormally small. Theobald, in a paper on "Subnormal Accommodative Power in Young Persons a not infrequent Cause of Asthenopia" says: "There is a condition which might, perhaps, be termed insufficiency of the ciliary muscles . . . It is met with not infrequently in different members of the same family, and is in many instances, no doubt, an *inherited* or *congenital defect.*"[2]

V. REFLEX ASTHENOPIA.—This is an eyestrain occurring in persons suffering from trouble, which indirectly affects the eyes, such as carious teeth, mental worry, uterine or sexual disorders. Jonathan Hutchinson, in a lecture delivered at Moorfields, in 1876, on the "Influence of the Sexual System on Diseases of the Eye,"[3] relates the case of a gentleman who suffered from accommodative asthenopia,

---

[1] *Oph. Rev.*, vol. vii., p. 26.
[2] *Trans. Am. Oph. Soc.*, vol. vi., part i., p. 127.
[3] R.L.O.H. Reports, vol. ix., p. 1.

which was due to excessive sexual abuse, and Fitzgerald relates the case of a young lady who suffered from asthenopia from the same cause.[1]

Pooley, in a paper on "The Relation of Uterine Disease to Asthenopia, and other affections of the Eye,"[2] cites several cases which prove conclusively, that the asthenopia that was suffered from was not due to any ocular defect, but to the reflex action of uterine or ovarian trouble.

Power has given a large number of instances, showing how the normal, or pathological condition of the sexual organs, may affect the eyes. He refers to the accommodative and muscular asthenopia produced in the young by sexual abuse, and also to the loss of accommodation observed during *pregnancy*. He says: "The patient finds herself unable to read or work for more than a few minutes; letters and lines run together; pain in the eye or brow—sometimes of an acute character—is felt, and the book is laid down not to be again taken up. This symptom, due to imperfect nutrition of the ciliary muscle and of the third nerve, probably depends on the watery state of the blood, and belongs to the same category as the vertigo and fainting that occasionally occur in pregnant women, *though it may be of a reflex nature*, and comparable with the amblyopia seen in cases of dental disease. The earliest period at which I have met with it has been at the eighth week, and in this case it occurred in a patient whose refraction was normal; but it is most common in the later months."[3]

Dysmenorrhœa sometimes produces symptoms of ciliary asthenopia in those whose refraction is emmetropic. Förster thinks that the failure of power is due to a reflex

---

[1] *Trans. Oph. Soc.*, vol. iii., p. 183.
[2] *New York Med. Journal*, February, 1886.
[3] *Trans. Oph. Soc.*, "Bowman Lecture," vol. viii., p. 24.

hyperæsthesia of the fifth nerve, and of the optic nerve. This " kopiopia hysterica " as it is called, is associated with hysterical symptoms, such as an exaggerated description of the complaints, and also with an intolerance to light, especially artificial light.

At the British Medical Association meeting in 1888, P. W. Maxwell read a paper on " *Chronic Nasal Catarrh*, as a reflex cause of Accommodative Asthenopia."[1] He stated that while the catarrh existed the asthenopia was present, and was only relieved by glasses, which could be discarded when the disease was cured.

And at the annual meeting of the American Ophthalmological Society, in 1886, Gruening stated that he found cases, complaining of irritation of the eyes and pain in the morning, unrelieved by glasses; that the trouble was due to *nasal* disease; and that out of two hundred cases treated on this supposition 150 had been benefited.[2]

Cheatham records three cases of asthenopia, which were only cured by treating the diseased nasal conditions.[3]

Rampoldi reports several cases of accommodative asthenopia due to reflex action, viz., hysteria, neuralgia of fifth nerve, *caries of teeth*, and as a sequel of an operation.[4]

Trousseau mentions cases of asthenopia cured by catheterising the lachrymal ducts.[5]

VI. TREATMENT.—*Methods of testing the sight.* Having placed our patient six metres in front of Snellen's test-types we record the vision in each eye separately, and if the sight is defective we also record the glass that improves

---

[1] *Oph. Rev.*, vol. vii., p. 305.
[2] *Oph. Rev.*, vol. v., p. 267.
[3] *Knapp's Archiv.*, vol. xvii., p. 124.
[4] *Knapp's Archiv.*, vol. xvii. p. 394.
[5] *Archives d'Ophth.*, vol. x., p. 183.

it. We then place Jaeger's reading type in the patient's hand, and again record in each eye separately the smallest type he can read, noting down the nearest and furthest point of his near vision, and if defective the glass that improves. In those under thirty years of age there is always more or less spasm of the ciliary muscle present, which sometimes masks the defect of vision and baulks the examination. To get rid of this we paralyse the accommodation. To produce this effect in the young it is necessary to drop into both eyes a solution of atropine (gr. iv. ad ʒj) three times a day for about a week, but as the effect of the atropine takes sometimes ten days to pass off, and as this is very inconvenient to older patients who may have their living to get, we can in them produce almost the same effect by dropping into the eye a solution of homatropine and cocaine in oil of sweet almonds or castor oil (gr. ii. of each to the ounce). One drop every five minutes for twenty minutes will generally produce the desired effect, and very often one drop only will be sufficient. The effect of the homatropine passes off generally in about thirty-six hours, although I have known it to take four days in an exceptional case.

Having by these means not only paralysed the accommodation but dilated the pupil, we take our patient into the dark room and by means of the "shadow test" or "keratoscopy" estimate the refraction. For the most lucid and exhaustive description of this method I refer the reader to a paper on the subject by Dr. Charnley.[1] Its chief value lies in the quickness and exactness of the results arrived at, as well as the absolute independence of the examiner, which we most appreciate when we are

---

[1] R.L.O.H. Reports, vol. x., p. 344.

dealing with nervous or stupid children, and of course it is most valuable in amblyopia or lessened visual acuteness in an eye. While in the dark room we take the opportunity of examining the eyes with the ophthalmoscope and noting any abnormality. If we are using a refraction ophthalmoscope we can corroborate our "keratoscopic" examination. Armed with this knowledge we again examine our patient before the test types, and note the vision and the glass required, if necessary, to improve it.

In patients over forty, as very little, if any spasm is present, we may dispense with a mydriatic, in fact it is best to do so because of the tendency to glaucoma that may be produced. In such case if we employ the "shadow test" we must direct the patient to gaze into distance, so as to ensure as much relaxation of the accommodation as possible.

Having satisfied ourselves that no error of refraction exists, and that we are dealing with an emmetrope, we find out the patient's habits or work. If our patient is a student or engaged in literary or other work that entails close application for many hours a day, and is free to regulate his work, we should advise working for shorter periods and with longer intervals of rest than he has been accustomed to. By daylight working with the window at his side, preferably the left, and at night using a lamp (which throws a good even white light on his work) with a green shade lined with white, so adjusted that no light from the lamp reaches the eyes directly. How often one finds students, by neglecting these details, impairing their health and breaking down at their examinations. The maximum time of close application to near work ought not to exceed eight hours a day. If a student or literary man were to regulate his work thus :—

Rise at 8	
Work from 9—12.30	3½ hours.
Outdoor exercise till 1.30	
Work from 2—3.30	1½ ,,
Spend rest of the afternoon in outdoor exercise till 6.30.	
Work from 8.30—11.30	3 ,,
	8 hours ;

he would in all probability never suffer from eyestrain if the eyes were normal. Persons engaged in any business or trade that requires close application of the eyes, may be greatly benefited by using weak convex glasses, say + 1 D., which have the effect not only of relieving the accommodation but also, as the retinal image is larger, of enabling the work to be removed further from the eyes, and so at the same time relieving the internal recti. The strain of these muscles, which we shall consider under muscular asthenopia, may be produced by the same cause as that which produces ciliary strain, viz., too close application of the eyes to the work, so that by giving them weak convex glasses, by one treatment we can cure two forms of strain. We thus see that it is most important to make the patient distinctly understand that he must on no account bring his work *nearer* to his eyes but if anything remove it further away.

We should also strongly advise these workers, to give their eyes complete rest when they have finished work, and whenever possible, to take out-door exercise which, at the same time that it improves the general health, also necessitates rest to the eye muscles.

Children whose eyesight is normal do not suffer from eyestrain, but as prevention is better than cure, careful attention to the ophthalmic hygiene of the school-room, may save them from much trouble in after years. This is

TREATMENT.

more important now in these days of universal education than it ever was, and if this matter is not attended to, we shall run the danger of becoming a nation of myopes like the Germans. The school-room should be lofty and large, and have large high windows on one wall. The seats and desks should be arranged in rows so that the pupils sit with the windows on their left. It is impossible of course to suit each pupil with seat and desk, but as most children of the same age are of the same height while sitting, and in the same class, the height of the desk from the seat should increase gradually with the classes, the highest class having the highest desks.

Priestley Smith has devised a "hygienic desk" and a table of the different sizes to suit all requirements, this table he has adapted and altered from one suggested by Snellen.[1]

If we have a uniform sized seat and desk for the whole school (which often happens), the youngest pupils are too near their work, and the oldest are too far away and have to stoop. When sitting at the desk, which should have a slight slope, the height of the seat should be such that the pupil can keep almost erect, and yet write comfortably at the same time.[2]

School books should be printed in a good type, uncramped. The printing of this book may be taken as a very fair sample of what the type of school books should be—of course the books for very young children must be printed in larger type.

Webster Fox in a paper on "Eyesight, its care during infancy and youth," has given ten rules to be observed for the preservation of vision.

---

[1] *Oph. Rev.*, vol. v., p. 160.
[2] *See* "The Hygiene of The Eye," by Cohn, chapter xi., and "The Causes and Prevention of Blindness," by Fuchs, section iii.

1. Do not allow light to fall upon the face of a sleeping infant.
2. Do not allow babies to gaze at a bright light.
3. Do not send children to school before the age of ten.
4. Do not allow children to keep their eyes too long on a near object, at any one time.
5. Do not allow them to study much by artificial light.
6. Do not allow them to use books with small type.
7. Do not allow them to read in a railway carriage.
8. Do not allow boys to smoke tobacco, especially cigarrettes.
9. Do not necessarily ascribe headaches to indigestion; the eyes may be the exciting cause.
10. Do not allow the spectacle vendor to prescribe glasses.

And last but not least, let us beware of overtaxing the child's brain, and as almost a necessary consequence, the eyesight as well. Day says: "The weakening more and more of the overtaxed brain lays the foundation of nerve exhaustion, and disorders are induced which years may never overcome,"[1] and he specially remarks on the harm done by teachers and parents by pushing a precocious child. The school work that needs close application of the eyes should be continued only for a short period at a time, the periods being well interspersed by other work, such as mental arithmetic or recitation, &c., which do not require the use of the eyes, and play.

I cannot leave the subject of eyestrain in the healthy, without referring to smoking. Apart from the harm that excessive smoking may do, by causing tobacco amblyopia, dyspepsia, &c., the eyes may suffer from direct contact with

---

[1] "Headaches," 1888, p. 339.

the smoke, and this temporary irritation may lead to permanent trouble in the shape of conjunctivitis, which would of course, render the eyes more liable to strain. All those, therefore, that have a tendency to eyestrain, should avoid smoking while at work; and if eyestrain is present, smoking *indoors* should be forbidden, and it might even be necessary to forbid it altogether until the eyes have quite recovered.

Those who have lost accommodative power by the drain on the system produced by a long illness or lactation, &c., should be given some form of tonic, such as iron and strychnia, Parrish's Food, Syrup of the Hypophosphites or Easton's Syrup, &c., and at the same time, they should be told to gradually and systematically exercise their ciliary muscle. Complete rest to the accommodation is a mistake, because through lack of sufficient exercise, the muscle will tend to become weaker still.

The weakened muscle should be carefully strengthened, by allowing the patient to read only for a prescribed time each day, which time is gradually, and, in some cases *very* gradually, increased until the cure is effected. This treatment was first advocated by Dyer, of Pittsburg, and is called "dyerising" in the United States. The patient may also carry about with him a concave glass, of say 8 D, and, at intervals during the day, look through this at distant objects (Collins). Most strict injunctions should be given that, except during the time that the eyes are being thus exercised, they should not be used for any other near work. The best plan is to direct the patient to begin by reading for five minutes three times a day, and when this can be done without any sign of fatigue, the time may be increased by a minute each day, until the patient can read for a quarter-of-an-hour three times a day without fatigue, this should be continued for a week, and then the time gradually increased again. No increase of time should ever be allowed while any symptoms of eyestrain remain.

When congenital subnormal accommodative power exists, weak convex glasses will remove the asthenopia if present. In reflex asthenopia we should, if possible, remove the cause. Until this is effected we may temporarily give weak convex glasses for near work.

Constitutional Treatment.—I cannot but think that there is a great tendency for Ophthalmologists to be too "special," to treat the eyes and their appendages as if they were isolated organs, and to ignore the immense influence that the constitutional condition has upon them. One ought to make it a practice never to treat the simplest eye affection without inspecting the tongue, and enquiring as to the state of the bowels. Many a patient may be cured of asthenopia by simply correcting some trouble of the stomach, liver, or bowels. Outdoor exercise and fresh air are absolutely essential for the maintenance of the physical well-being of the individual, and we should never lose an opportunity of impressing this fact upon those that have to work in a vitiated atmosphere.

Illustrative Cases. — *Eyestrain with normal sight.*— Abuse :—

H. D., a printer, aged 23, complains of pain and inflammation in the eyes. His work is chiefly at night, and consequently, by artificial light, and he says that when he has finished work, the eyes are much worse.

He has slight conjunctivitis, and marked chronic blepharitis. He sees $\frac{6}{6}$ with each eye, and has no hyperopia; his near point is 13 cms. from the eyes, showing an accommodative power of 7.5 D. He converges easily to 10 cms., and "Maddox rod test" shows no latent divergence. This is a case of simple ciliary strain; working constantly by artificial light and at fine work, he has abused his ciliary muscles. He was advised to abstain from all near work when off duty, and to take as much outdoor exercise as possible.

Neuropathic Asthenopia.—Lactation.

Mrs. R. R., aged 34, has had six children, the last, eighteen months ago. She has suckled the child all this time.

She says she sees all right "about," but if she takes up a book to read or something to sew, "everything goes into one." She does not see double.

If she tries to read or sew she gets a bad headache. The pain is mostly occipital, and very often ocular.

$$\frac{RV}{LV} > -\tfrac{8}{8} + .5\,D = Hm. \qquad P = 33 \text{ cms.} \quad \therefore a = 3.5\,D.$$

At her age her amplitude of accommodation should be 5.5 D (see page 59).

Advised to wean the child, and ordered to wear glasses +1 D for near work until stronger.

VII. CILIARY STRAIN IN AMETROPIA.—This is the *Accommodative Asthenopia* of most writers, and is due to fatigue of the ciliary muscle through its attempt to overcome some error of refraction, by causing the lens to assume such form, that the image of an object shall be focussed on the retina.

Donders taught that the hypermetropic structure of the eye was, almost without exception, the only cause of accommodative asthenopia or ciliary strain, but we shall see that astigmatism may also be a cause from unequal demand in the one eye, or anisometropia from unequal demand in the two eyes, and finally presbyopia from the diminished power of accommodation, owing to the lessened elasticity of the lens. The symptoms of ciliary strain are in many cases due to the altered relations between the efforts of accommodation and convergence, the former being used in excess of the latter.

It is hardly necessary to point out that if the various conditions exist, which we have seen may give rise to asthenopia in the emmetropic eye, all the more likely are we to find strain present in the ametropic eye.

VIII. ACCOMMODATION.

Accommodation is the change in the convexity of the lens brought about by the action of the ciliary muscle. The frontispiece is a diagrammatic section of an eye, showing the mechanism of accommodation.

According to Iwanoff, the ciliary muscle arises from a tendinous ring (t) close to the insertion of the iris and Schlemm's canal (c.s.), at the posterior surface of the sclerotic, close to its junction with the cornea. The muscle then passes backwards and may be divided into three parts, (1) the outermost part or meridional portion passing into the posterior tendon (m) to be inserted into the choroid, (2) the radiating portion (r), and (3) the annular portion or circular muscle of Müller (c) passing directly backwards and inwards respectively, to be inserted into an agglomeration of fibres called the zone of Zinn (z). These fibres arise partly from the ciliary portion of the retina at the ora serrata (o.s.) and partly from the ciliary processes and the intervals between them and they pass forwards and backwards to be inserted into the anterior and posterior capsule of the lens. When the ciliary muscle contracts it pulls forwards and inwards the zone of Zinn, and by this mechanism the compression exercised by the latter on the lens is relaxed, and the lens is allowed by virtue of its elastic fibres to assume a more convex form, producing the same effect on rays passing through it, as if a convex glass were placed in front of the eye, and this effect is to bring forward the focal point of the rays, so that an object that was previously focussed behind the retina can now be focussed on it. When the ciliary muscle relaxes, the zone of Zinn again compresses the lens, which resumes its less convex shape. At the same time that the ciliary muscle contracts, the circular fibres of the iris also contract, and we get the pupil diminished in size. Both the ciliary muscle and the circular fibres of the iris are supplied by fibres from the third nerve.

Amplitude of Accommodation.—At rest the eye is adapted for the most distant point it can see distinctly, viz., its *punctum remotum* R, while the greatest possible contraction of the ciliary muscle adapts the eye to the nearest point it can see distinctly, viz., its *punctum proximum* P, which represents the greatest possible contraction. The force required to change the eye from R to P is called the amplitude of accommodation and is represented by the *difference* between the refraction of the eye at rest and the refraction when doing its utmost work. The equation is:—

$$a = p - r$$

where "a" equals the number of dioptres represented by the accommodation, "p" equals the number of dioptres represented by the eye when in a state of maximum refraction, *i.e.*, when adapted for its nearest distinct point, and "r" equals the number of dioptres represented by the eye at rest, *i.e.*, when adapted for its furthest distinct point.

In *Emmetropia* as R is at infinity

$$a = p - \infty = p - o = p$$

therefore the amplitude of accommodation is represented by the nearest distinct point, if this is 9 cms. off 'a' = $\frac{100}{9}$ = 11 D—that is, the power of accommodation this person possesses is equal to a lens of eleven dioptres.

In myopia "r" has a positive value. Take for example, a person whose furthest distinct point with the eye at rest is 33 cms. (that is a myope of 3 D), and suppose that his nearest distinct point is 7 cms., then

$$\begin{aligned} a &= p - r \\ &= \tfrac{100}{7} - \tfrac{100}{33} \\ &= 14 - 3 \\ &= 11\ D \end{aligned}$$

In other words, 14 D would represent his amplitude of accommodation if he were emmetropic, but being myopic to the extent of 3 D we must subtract that, which leaves us 11 D to represent his amplitude.

In hyperopia, as we shall see later, "r" is negative, therefore the equation is:—

$$a = p - (-r)$$
$$= p + r$$

Thus, an eye hyperopic to the extent of 5 D, having its near point at 25 cms. from the eye, has an amplitude of accommodation equal to a lens 9 D.

To see 25 cms. off the eye requires an accommodation of 4 D ($\frac{100}{25}$), but it has already expended 5 D for distance, so that

$$a = p - (-r)$$
$$= 4 - (-5)$$
$$= 4 + 5 = 9 \text{ D}$$

We thus see that to determine the amplitude or range of accommodation we must find R and P.

R is represented by the refraction of the eye at rest.

P we find as follows:—

Take a tape, graduated on one side in centimetres, and on the other in corresponding dioptres. The zero-end of the tape is attached to the handle of a frame, into which may be introduced either a perforated diaphragm, or a paper with fine print upon it, or threads or hairs. This frame is brought towards the eye that is being examined (the other one being covered), until the objects begin to appear indistinct, we then read off on the tape the distance of P from the eye, and the corresponding dioptres (p) representing the maximum refractive power of the eye (Landolt).

If from any cause, such as presbyopia or high hyper-

metropia, the patient's near point is so far that the above tests cannot be employed, we place up in front of the eye such a convex glass that will bring the punctum proximum (P) closer and enable him to read J1, or see the words, &c., in the frame, such glass to be, of course, deducted afterwards. Thus, supposing a person with $+2$ can bring the test object up to 25 cms. and no nearer, we read off on the other side of the tape 4 D, and we substract the $+2$ from this which gives us $p = 2$ D, that is, P is 50 centimetres off; if he is an emmetropic presbyope, this represents his amplitude of accommodation; but if, say, he is hyperopic to the extent of 6 D, then $a = 2 + 6$
$$= 8 \text{ D}$$
or suppose the patient being hyperopic and presbyopic, requires $+5$ D to read at 33 cms. If his hyperopia $= 6$ D, then
$$a = p + r$$
$$= (3 - 5) + 6$$
$$= 4 \text{ D}$$

We may find the amplitude of accommodation another way.

First we ascertain the static refraction; if the patient is emmetropic we put up before the eyes concave glasses, and the strongest concave glass he can see with at a distance, distinctly represents his amplitude of accommodation. Thus if -9 D is the strongest glass he can bear, he has 9 D amplitude of accommodation. If he is myopic we proceed in the same way but deduct the amount of myopia. Thus if -9 is the strongest concave that can be borne and the myopia amounts to 2 D, $9 - 2 = 7 =$ amplitude of accommodation. In hyperopia we *add* the number of the strongest concave glass to the amount of hyperopia. Thus if with -8 D he can see distance distinctly and his hyperopia is 2 D, $8 + 2 = 10 =$ amplitude of accommodation. In cases where a hyperope can stand no concave glass we must find the *weakest* convex glass with which he can see well at a distance, and the difference between that and the total hyperopia gives the amplitude of accommodation, for if the strongest concave glass gives the refraction of the eye when at rest, the weakest convex glass will give the maximum refraction obtained by accommodation. This method, though apparently so simple, has drawbacks. The retinal image is very small, and so visual acuteness suffers and it requires on the part of the patient a certain amount of intelligence and also of education of his ciliary muscles not always possessed, especially by the young.

IX. THE INFLUENCE OF AGE UPON THE ACCOMMODATION.—*Presbyopia:* (πρέσβυς old, ὤψ eye). The amplitude of accommodation diminishes with age.

At the age of 10 years the average emmetrope's near

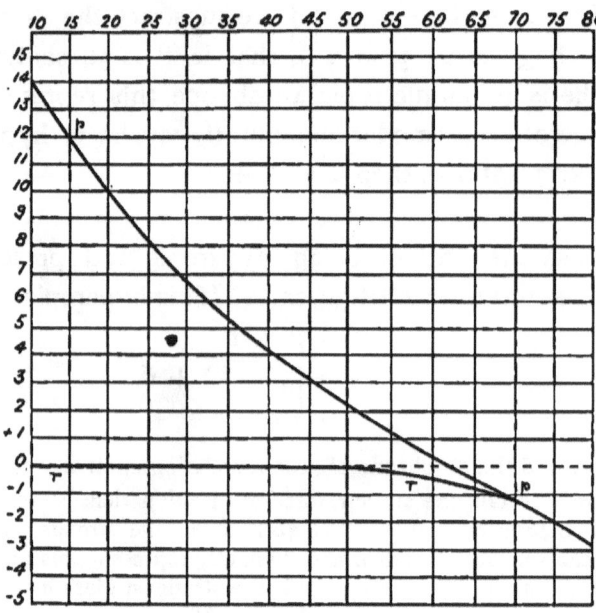

FIG. 3.

The figures above, represent years, those on the left, dioptres. The line p p, represents the curve of the Punctum Proximum, and the line r r, that of the Punctum Remotum (Landolt).

point is seven centimetres from the eye, and his far point being at infinity we see that his amplitude of accommodation is 14 D (fig. 3), whereas at the age of 30, his near point has receded to 14 cms., and his amplitude of accommodation is then only 7 D, that is, in twenty years he has lost half of his accommodative power.

INFLUENCE OF AGE UPON THE ACCOMMODATION. 57

The same happens, whatever the refractive condition of the eye, for instance, a hyperope of 4 D (fig. 4) at the age of 10, has his near point ten centimetres from the eye and $p = \frac{1 \text{ metre}}{P} = \frac{100}{10} = 10$ D, "r" is negative, and we have

$$a = 10 - (-4)$$
$$= 10 + 4$$
$$= 14 \text{ D}$$

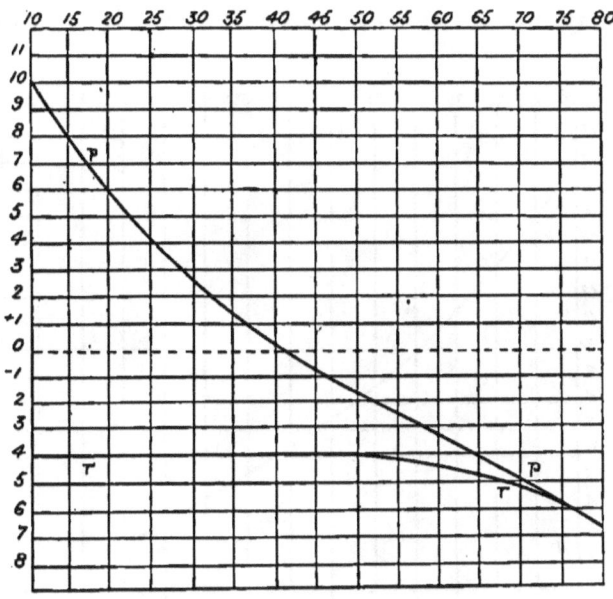

FIG. 4.

Again, at 30 we see (fig. 4) that $p = 3$ D, P being now 33 centimetres from the eye, and we have

$$a = 3 + 4$$
$$= 7 \text{ D}$$

A myope, say of 3 D (fig. 5) has his near point at the age of ten, 6 cms. from the eye, and $p = 17$ D

$$a = 17 - 3$$
$$= 14 \text{ D}$$

At the age of thirty, we see by the diagram that $p = 10$ D for $P = 10$ cms., and R is still 33 cms. on the positive side, hence

$$a = p - r$$
$$= 10 - 3$$
$$= 7 \text{ D}$$

Whatever the static refraction of the eye is, "r" remains stationary till about the age of 55, when we see that in all three diagrams it begins to curve downwards, showing that

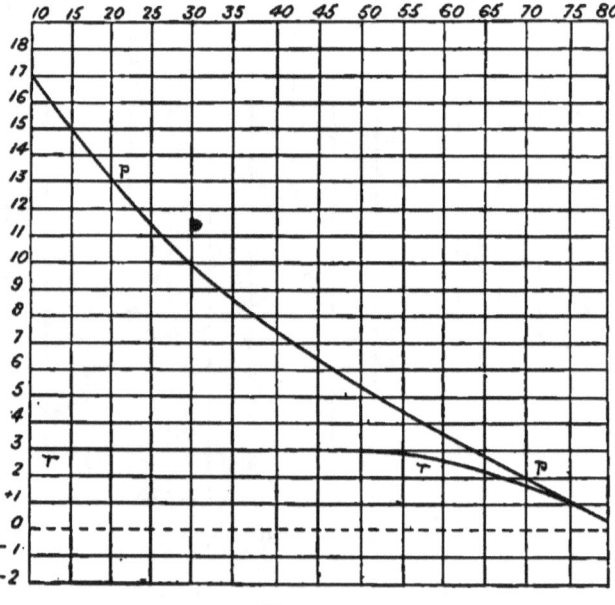

FIG. 5.

the emmetrope becomes hyperopic, the hyperope more so, and the myope less so. A point is finally reached when "p" and "r" unite, in other words, when all accommodation ceases; this is about the age of 75, according to Landolt; but in emmetropia and hyperopia, the positive part of accommodation, viz., that employed for near objects,

INFLUENCE OF AGE UPON THE ACCOMMODATION.

ceases at an earlier age. In emmetropia "p" is seen to cross the zero line between the ages of 60 and 65 (fig. 3) (some accommodation is still left, but it is employed in correcting the "acquired hyperopia"), and in hyperopia even earlier. The greater the degree of hyperopia, the earlier will "p" cross the zero line. In the case of a hyperope of 4 D (fig. 4), this happens between the ages of 40 and 45. That is, a hyperope of 4 D when he reaches the age of 42, although he has some amplitude of accommodation, has to use it up entirely for distance; on the other hand, all myopes of more than 3 D can make use of all the accommodative powers they have, for near work (fig. 5). These conclusions were arrived at by Donders, from a number of observations made and recorded,[1] and fig. 3 is the result of the averages of these observations.

By referring to fig. 3 we get the following table:—
Every person ought to have at

Age.	Range of accommodation.
10	14 Dioptres
15	12 ,,
20	10 ,,
25	8.5 ,,
30	7 ,,
35	5.5 ,,
40	4.5 ,,
45	3.5 ,,
50	2.5 ,,
55	1.75 ,,
60	1 ,,
65	.75 ,,
70	.25 ,,
75	0 ,,

[1] "Accommodation and Refraction of the Eye," p. 209.

It is very important to remember, that this table is only meant to show the average standard. In practice we often find considerable variation from it.

This loss of accommodative power in the eye is due to diminished elasticity of the lens—in other words, the greatest convexity the lens can assume is at the age of 10; and every year afterwards, this convexity (which is the result of the fullest relaxation of the zone of Zinn) becomes less and less, till a time arrives, when it has lost all power of altering in shape.

This loss of elasticity is accompanied by greater firmness of the lens, and in later years, by a loss of homogeneousness and transparency both of the lens and vitreous, which is such a striking condition in youth. The lens reflects more light, and by oblique illumination often gives a false idea of cataract. At the age of 40 every individual has, more or less, about 4.5 D. range of accommodation (see table). From our formula $a = p - r$ we get $p = a + r$, *i.e.* $p = 4.5 + r$. If the person is an emmetrope $r = \infty = 0$ $\therefore$ $p = 4.5$; now P. the punctum proximum is $\frac{1 \text{ metre}}{p.}$ therefore $P = \frac{1 \text{ metre}}{4.5} = 22$cms. That is, an emmetrope at the age of 40 cannot read distinctly nearer than 22cms. or $8\frac{1}{2}$ inches. This is the point at which Donders has fixed presbyopia. At what age will a myope of 2 D. have his near point removed to 22cms.?

$$a = p - r$$
$$= 4.5 - 2$$
$$= 2.5$$

By our table we see that, when the amplitude of accommodation has diminished to 2.5, the person's age is 50. Hence a myope of 2 D. becomes presbyopic ten years later than an emmetrope. If the amount of myopia had been 4.5 D. "a" would have been 0, and our table shows us that the age when all accommodation is lost is 75. The myope, who all his life has never seen clearly without glasses, beyond a point eight inches from his nose, has this solitary compensation, that he will be able to read without glasses up to, and beyond, the natural term of life.

As we have seen, a hyperope becomes presbyopic earlier than an emmetrope or myope.

At what age will a hyperope of 4 D. become presbyopic, that is have his near point removed to 22cms.?

$$a = p - (-r)$$
$$= p + r$$
$$= 4.5 + 4$$
$$= 8.5$$

Our table shows us that a person having an amplitude of accommodation of 8.5 D. is 25 years old. It seems rather cruel to tell a young lady of 25 who is hyperopic to the extent of 4 D., that she is just commencing to suffer from "old sight"! Although it may be somewhat soothing to inform her, that everyone really begins to suffer from it at the early age of ten.

Some writers object to the term "presbyopia," and would expunge it from ophthalmology, giving us nothing in its place. We must have some term to express that "condition in which, as the result of the increase of years, the range of accommodation is diminished and the vision of near objects is interfered with" (Donders).

It certainly seems rather arbitrary to say, as Donders does, that presbyopia commences when P. has receded to 22cms. from the eye, but this can do no harm if we bear in mind the fact, that the presence of presbyopia does not necessarily entail the use of glasses for near work. As Landolt says, a long armed man would not thank you to bring his near work so close to his eyes as 22cms.

The recognition of presbyopia is not difficult. If a person complains that he has to hold his book when reading further away than he has been accustomed to do, that this is more especially so by artificial light, that the figures 3, 5 and 8 become confused and that n and u are difficult to distinguish, and at the same time, he asserts that his distant vision has not altered, we may be almost certain we have before us a presbyope.

If a person whose near point has receded, say, to 33 cms., attempts to read or work at that distance for any length of time, symptoms of eyestrain will be sure to supervene.

It is a fact that we get from everyday experience, that the full power of a muscle can only be exercised for a very short time without fatigue. A person whose near point is at 33 cms. is using the whole powers of his ciliary muscle, in order to focus an object at that distance on his retina, and fatigue of the muscle will very soon ensue. This fatigue causes the muscle to relax, it cannot contract to its full extent, vision then becomes hazy, and only becomes distinct again, when the object has been further removed from the eye. At the same time, the patient will probably complain that after reading some little time, headache comes on, and the eyes begin to water; these temporary symptoms of eyestrain will pass into chronic symptoms in time, and the red, irritable-looking, watery eyes of middle-aged people are often due to this cause.

There is no doubt that presbyopia is a very fertile cause of eyestrain. I find, on referring to my own cases, that no less than 38.9 per cent. of presbyopes suffered from *accommodative asthenopia*.

Day, in his work on "Headaches," refers to the fact that women at the climacteric, that is about the age of 45, often suffer from headache, which he classes as "*nervo-hyper-*

æmic"[1]; as this is commonly the age of presbyopia, it is possible that many "*climacteric*" headaches are the result of eyestrain, through the presbyope overtaxing her weakened accommodative power. Again, although the headache may not be actually caused by the eyestrain, the latter may start an attack in one predisposed.

Treatment of Presbyopia.—Two classes of patients come to us for treatment under this heading; one class, mostly hospital patients, simply request glasses for reading (many of these have been to various opticians and been unsuited, and we very often find them suffering from incipient cataract); the other class come complaining of some symptom of asthenopia, and they may, or may not, be aware that they require glasses.

A mydriatic is not necessary (except in isolated cases where our results are unsatisfactory, and we wish to thoroughly examine the lens for cataract), ciliary spasm is very unlikely to be present, and latent hyperopia, if it has been present is becoming, or has become, manifest, and we avoid the danger of glaucoma, which has sometimes been traced to the employment of atropine.

We first test the patient's distant vision, and then find his near point of distinct vision, and also ascertain from him his usual or most comfortable distance for reading or working at.

Suppose his distant vision is normal, and his punctum proximum is 28 cms., and the distance he wishes to read at is 33 cms.; he complains, we will say, of symptoms of eyestrain, how can we relieve him?

His amplitude of accommodation is $\frac{100}{28} = 3.5$ D. Now, to avoid fatigue, he must not use the whole of this, but

---

[1] *Op. cit.*, p. 251.

must keep about ⅓ in reserve. Let him have 1.5 D. in reserve, this leaves him 2 D. available accommodative power, but to work at 33 cms. he requires 3 D. We supply this deficit by giving him + 1 D. glasses to work with. He suffered from eyestrain, because he was using almost the whole of his accommodative power.

The treatment, simple as it appears, is not always successful, because the amount of reserve accommodation left, is not always large enough. It necessarily varies with the individual. If the ciliary muscle is weak, we must leave a larger reserve and *vice versâ*.

Most people put off "taking to spectacles" as long as possible, because it is considered a sign of *old* age (ladies especially are very great delinquents in this respect), and when, after suffering eyestrain for years, nature forces them to find relief in glasses they seek the advice of an optician who, with very few exceptions, is not competent to thoroughly examine the sight.

Persons should remember that convex glasses, even if worn too soon, can never do anything like the harm that eyestrain does.

We can quite understand that chronic eyestrain in presbyopia may be one of the causes of cataract. The ciliary strain produces a series of phenomena both in the vascular and nervous system, which may easily interfere with the nutrition of the lens.

On the other hand, Donders says, "So long as the eye does not err, and remains free from fatigue in the work required of it, its own power is sufficient, and it is inexpedient to seek assistance in the use of convex glasses."[1]

We generally find in practice, that an emmetrope of 45

---

[1] *Op. cit.*, p. 219.

requires a convex glass of 1 D., and an additional + 1 D. for every additional five years.

If any error of refraction is present, that must be ascertained; the patient should then be supplied with the correcting glasses, thus making him, more or less, emmetropic; and the rest of the examination should be proceeded with as before, the convex glass that his presbyopia requires being added to the correcting glasses.

Thus, if the patient is hyperopic to the extent of 3 D., and we find by our examination that he requires an additional 1 D. to work with, we order + 4 D. for near work. If he is myopic to the extent of 1 D. and requires an additional + 2 D. to read with, we add the negative glass to this, and then give him + 1 D. for near work; and so with astigmatism.

Illustrative cases. *Accommodative Asthenopia in simple Presbyopia.*

G. H., 43. An engraver, complains of aching of eyes and head. Has chronic conjunctivitis, says that his chief work is engraving armorial bearings and crests and that he sometimes works twelve hours a day, and never uses a watchmaker's glass. His accommodative near point is 22 cms. and he generally works at about 25 cms. He has no error of refraction . . . a = 4.5. His convergence n ar point is 7 cms., he has no latent deviation for distance . . . his ca = 14 ma. Working at 25 cms. he employs almost the whole of his accommodative power and has too little in reserve, but he has a large amount of convergence power in reserve. He is advised to use convex glasses of 1 D. when at work. He ought to keep one third of his accommodative power in reserve, *i.e.*, $\frac{1}{3}$ × 4.5, = 1.5, this then leaves him with + 3 D. and to work at 25 cms. he requires + 4 D., therefore by giving him + 1 D. we supply the deficiency.

Accommodative Asthenopia—Neurasthenia, Presbyopia, Hyperopia.

Mrs. A. B., an artist, aged 35, complains that all near work produces after a short time, dimness of sight, pain in the eyes, and headache. The time she has been able to work "at a stretch" has been getting shorter and shorter, and has reached the point now when she positively dreads using her eyes for any close work, as the distressing symptoms supervene at once. She fears that there is some serious disease of the eyes; of late years she has overworked a great deal and her nervous system has thoroughly broken down.

$$\begin{matrix} R & V \\ L & V \end{matrix} > \tfrac{4}{7} \text{ Hm} + .5 \text{ D.} ; P = 22 \text{ cms.} \therefore a = 4.5 + .5 = 5 \text{ D.}$$

and as she often works at 25 cms. she is keeping too little accommodation in reserve. Ophthalmoscope reveals nothing—the recti normal. This is a clear case of accommodative asthenopia produced by three different agents, viz., diminished accommodation due to (1) age, (2) lessened neuro-muscular power, (3) undue strain.

Advised to suspend all work at present, to put herself under her medical adviser with the view of improving her general health, and to gradually begin near work after Dr. Dyer's method, using $+$ 1 D. glasses.

Asthenopia—Presbyopia—Myopia.

Mrs. S. G., aged 60, complains of sore eyes, has chronic blepharitis. Frontal headache after reading or sewing. Eyes very often pain at back. Has never worn glasses. The eyes have been more painful and more easily fatigued since an attack of "influenza."

$$\begin{matrix} R & V \\ L & V \end{matrix} > \tfrac{6}{30} - 1.5 \text{ D.} = \tfrac{4}{7}$$

$$P = 33 \text{ cms.}$$

She was given Franklin glasses, the upper half being $-$ 1.5 D. in both eyes and the lower half $+$ 1.5 D. Seen some months later all asthenopic symptoms had disappeared.

X. Another cause of eyestrain is **HYPEROPIA** ($\Upsilon\pi\acute{\epsilon}\rho$, in excess, $\grave{\omega}\psi$, eye) or hypermetropia. The hyperopic eye is the flat, or undeveloped eye, in which with accommodation at rest, parallel rays come to a focus beyond the retina (fig. 6 H), and only convergent rays focus on the retina; but in nature all rays are either parallel or divergent, so that the hyperopic eye at rest sees everything indistinctly.

The punctum remotum of a hyperope is beyond infinity; it is the point towards which the luminous rays ought to converge in order to be focussed on the retina, hence it is *behind* the eye, and is therefore represented as negative, viz., $-$ R (fig. 7), being the virtual and not the actual focus of the distant rays.

HYPEROPIA.

There are three causes of hyperopia—

1.—Axial hyperopia. This is the most usual form; it is due to the shortening of the antero-posterior axis, the

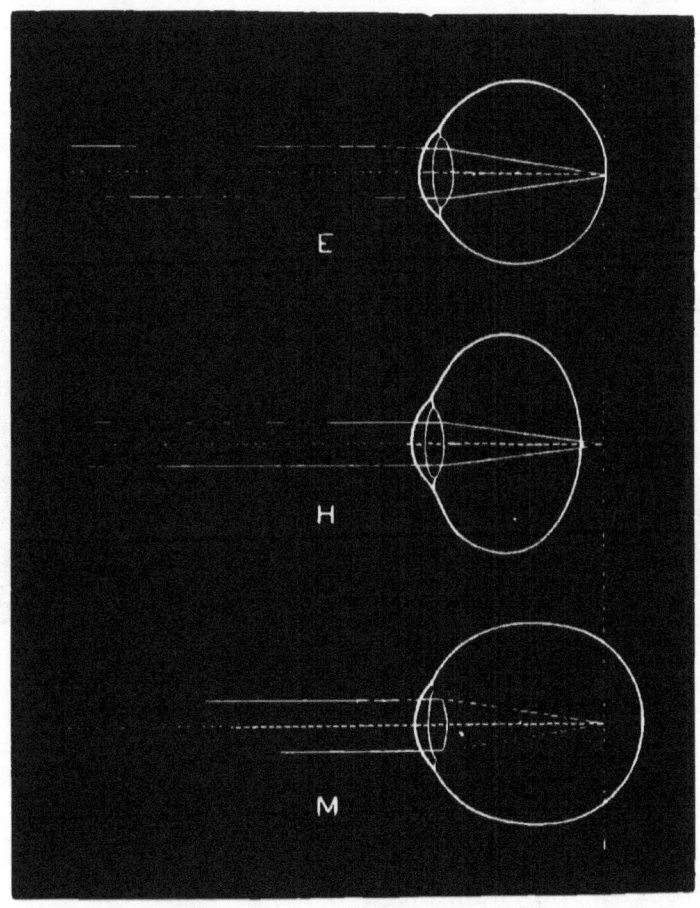

FIG. 6.

Showing parallel rays focussed on the retina in Emmetropia (E), behind the retina in Hyperopia (H), and in front of the retina in Myopia (M).

dioptric system being as powerful as in an emmetropic eye. This is owing to an arrest of growth of the eye and is very often associated with the arrest of growth of the bony parts surrounding; thus, the face of a hyperope often shows a want of relief.

2.—Curvature hyperopia, due to a lack of convexity of the refractive surfaces. This is the form in hyperopic astigmatism; and

3.—Hyperopia from a change in the index of refraction, due to decrease in that of the aqueous humour and lens, and increase in that of the vitreous humour.

Axial hyperopia is far the commonest, so that we may say generally, that a hyperopic eye is a flat eye.

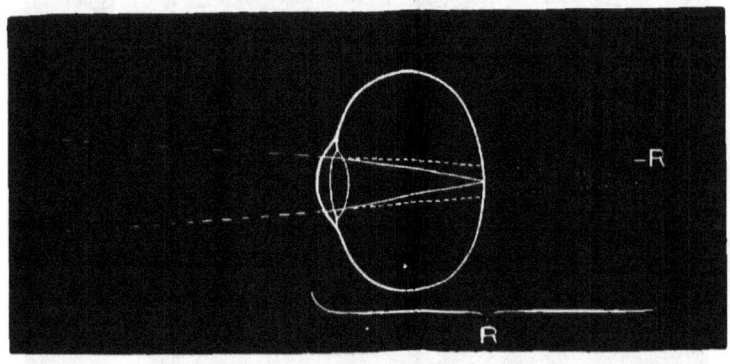

FIG. 7.
Showing the punctum remotum of a hyperopic eye.

The hyperope, to remedy his defect, must accommodate for distance, as well as for near objects, and this explains at once, the reason why eyestrain is so commonly met with, in persons suffering from this defect.

Out of a total of 2,316 patients who have come under my care, suffering from some error of refraction, no less than 518 were hyperopic, and a very large percentage of these suffered from eyestrain. Selecting the private cases (where full notes were taken), 39 per cent. of hyperopes suffered from eyestrain (see page 29).

HYPEROPIA.

The emmetrope's ciliary muscle is at rest when he is looking at anything beyond twenty feet, but the hyperope's eye is never at rest if he attempts to see distinctly; and, moreover, when he wishes to look at a near object, he starts with a deficit, which deficit is the amount of accommodation he required for distant vision. Thus, a hyperope of four dioptres with five dioptres of accommodation, can focus distant objects clearly, but then he has only *one* dioptre left for near vision, this will only bring his near point to one metre from the eyes. Again, take a hyperope of two dioptres with five dioptres of accommodation, he only has three

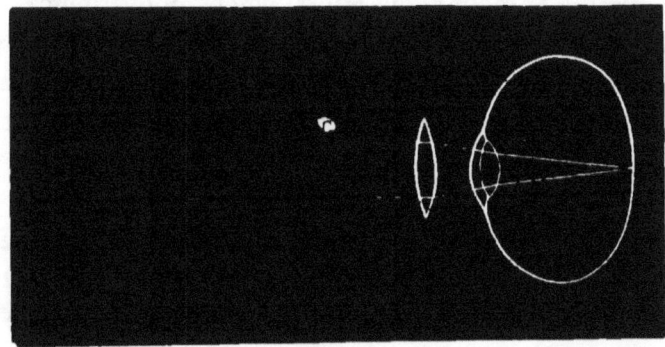

FIG. 8.

Showing parallel rays focussed on the retina of a hyperopic eye by means of a convex lens.

dioptres available for accommodation of near objects, this brings his near point to 33 cms., but he is using the whole of his accommodative power for this, and it is impossible for him to do this for long, without fatigue, and so we get all the symptoms of eyestrain.

The want of harmony between the accommodative and convergence efforts, is another cause of eyestrain in hyperopia.

In our last example we see that the hyperope of 2 D., when looking at a point 33 cms. off, is using 5 D. of accommodation, but he only requires to use 3-metre angles of convergence (see Part III.), therefore he is using 2 D. of accommodative power in excess of convergence. Now nature has endowed many hyperopes with the power of increasing their accommodation, *to a certain extent*, without varying their convergence; this faculty is the result of "nerve education." We shall see when dealing with muscular asthenopia, that the same thing occurs in myopia, only in this case it is the convergence that is strained, because it is in excess of the accommodation. There is a minimum amount of effort when convergence and accommodation work harmoniously together, as it were supporting each other, but when one is used in excess of the other, it has to work unaided and alone, and strain is liable to ensue.

Many hyperopes never learn this trick, as we may call it, of using their accommodation in excess of convergence, and therefore they are less likely to suffer from strain (although the unconscious effort to do so may induce it); but a worse evil befalls them, they lose binocular vision, and squint. A hyperope under these circumstances finds himself in the following dilemma: If he wants to see binocularly, he must use less accommodative power than he requires to see distinctly; or if he wishes to see distinctly he must sacrifice binocular vision, which ends in squint. He must choose between distinct vision and binocular vision. Distinct vision is more craved for, and more useful than binocular vision, especially if the latter is not quite perfect owing to one eye being more defective than the other; consequently he sacrifices binocular vision and squints. The dilemma ends and asthenopia ceases;

naturally before this final result is reached the struggle must cause strain.

A hyperope of high degree is very badly off, for he cannot obtain clear images by any contrivance; he thus avoids accommodative asthenopia, but runs the risk of suffering from muscular asthenopia (convergence strain), through approaching his eyes too near to his work, in order to obtain large retinal images.

The hyperopia which is at once recognized, the patient at once confessing to improved vision with a convex glass, is called manifest; this manifest hyperopia (Hm) is expressed in amount by the *strongest* convex glass the patient can take; for instance a patient sees $\frac{6}{9}$ but with $+$ 1 D. up in front of the eye $\frac{6}{8}$, and $+$ 1.5 D. makes the letters hazy, then $+$ 1 D. $=$ Hm. The latent hyperopia is the additional hyperopia, which shows itself when the accommodation has been relaxed with atropine. If the patient quoted above, when under atropine, sees $\frac{6}{8}$ only when $+$ 3 D. is put up, in his case $+$ 2 D. represents the latent hyperopia, Hl, the total hyperopia, Ht, being the sum of Hm and Hl. Hm $+$ Hl $=$ Ht. Donders further divides Hm into

(1) *Absolute hyperopia*, when, with the strongest convergence of visual lines, accommodation for parallel or converging rays cannot be attained, the focus always lying behind the retina, and a convex glass always being required for distant vision.

(2) *Relative hyperopia*, when parallel rays can be brought to a focus on the retina by accommodation and convergence, the latter being in excess of the amount of convergence required. To accommodate for a near point the patient must converge to a point still nearer, *i.e.*, to see clearly at 22 cms. he must converge, say, for 12 cms., in other words he squints.

(3) *Facultative hyperopia,* when the focus of parallel rays can be brought to the retina by accommodation alone and objects at a distance can be accurately seen with or without convex glasses.

Landolt divides manifest hyperopia into (1) absolute manifest hyperopia (H ma) which no effort of the accommodation can conceal and which is represented by the weakest convex glass that gives the greatest visual acuteness, and (2) facultative manifest hyperopia (H mf) which the patient can correct at will and is represented by the difference between the strongest and weakest glass which gives him the best distant vision. Thus a hyperope of 5 D. may be made up as follows :

$$Hl = 2\ D.$$
$$Hm = Hmf = 1$$
$$Hma = 2$$
$$= 3\ D.$$
$$Ht = 5\ D.$$

Now it is this facultative hyperopia which the patient can correct, and thus more or less conceal, at will, that is one of the most common causes of eyestrain, and the reason is very apparent.

In absolute Hm, vision is never acute, and the patient makes no attempt to strain his accommodation, because he finds the result useless, more or less.

In relative Hm, we have seen that only monocular vision can be acute, and that asthenopia generally ceases when the squint appears, but in

Facultative Hm, patients are most frequently quite unaware that they are suffering from any defect of the eyes; they can see well at a distance and their near vision is as good as they want, and they have no idea that the headaches that come on after near work, are caused by eyestrain, and they will in all probability be treated for all manner of diseases before the real cause is discovered. It is true that if this eystrain goes on for long, signs of inflammation will often show themselves in the eye and its appendages, such as conjunctivitis and blepharitis, and lead the patient to the eye surgeon, but even he may miss the true cause, unless he makes it a rule (which he ought to) to examine the eye under atropine of all young people (and this is essentially a disease of the young) suffering from chronic inflammation of the lids or conjunctiva.

The facultative hyperopia of the young becomes in middle life relative, and after 50, absolute, so that although it is quite possible to suffer from facultative Hm, and pass through youth without any symptoms of eyestrain, sooner or later they will appear. Good health, plenty of outdoor exercise and not too much application to books, will ward off eyestrain for a long time, but in these days of examinations, the day must surely come, when the young student must "cram," when he must read four or five hours a day by artificial light, when he must put in more work and take less play—in other words, when he must use his muscles of accommodation for a much longer time. And now, after a few hours' reading, his head aches, his eyes pain, and the type runs together. Of course many such cases may occur from simple overwork in emmetropes, but I am confident that many a young man has broken down reading for his "Tripos" simply because he was hyperopic and had overstrained his eyes. I have known several men suffer from eyestrain for the first time through taking up German or Hebrew; the fine strokes that have to be recognised in order to distinguish the different letters (especially is this so in Hebrew), put an extra strain on the accommodation, and if the eye starts with a deficit, as it does in hyperopia, eyestrain is sure to ensue and we get all its attendant symptoms.

If symptoms of eyestrain occur amongst the upper

classes who suffer from this low form of hyperopia, how much more must they occur, in those who spend their lives at close work in badly lit and badly ventilated rooms, with little or no outdoor exercise, and often insufficient food, and yet the large army of seamstresses and compositors, etc., who find their way to the out-patient room of an ophthalmic hospital, are, I believe, only a small fraction of the number that really want relief, but do not recognise it, because they see well without glasses. Those who do come for advice generally tell the same tale; they are at work, say, with the needle from eight in the morning till eight or ten at night, and towards evening they complain that their vision becomes less acute, it is difficult to thread a needle, and their eyes and head ache. It is but natural; their ciliary muscles have been working at high pressure all day, and in their little way have done as much work as the leg muscles would in a 30-mile walk. Surely in an emmetropic eye we should expect fatigue under such circumstances; how much more then in hyperopia!

Now we ask what is the cause of this eyestrain in low hyperopia in the young, who have such a relatively large amount of accommodative power in reserve? A boy of 10 with 2 D. hyperopia has still 12 D. of accommodative power, which brings his near point to 8 cms. where he will never have to work. At 22 cms., the ordinary working point, he is using only 4.5 D. of the 12 D., and has 7.5 D. accommodative power in reserve! The explanation of this is, firstly, although we take, according to Donders, our typical emmetrope of 10 as having 14 D. of accommodation, like all types, many fall short of this, and it is these exceptions that find their way to the eye surgeon. In my own experience I find the *exception* is to get a patient having the standard accommodative power. Secondly, it is a very common and bad habit for children to read and work, with the object held too near the eyes (see p. 36). This will still more reduce the accommodation held in reserve, and it is important to remember that to avoid fatigue about one-third should be held in reserve (Landolt). For instance, supposing we find a young hyperope of 2 D. has only 9 D. of amplitude of accommodation, he ought only to use 6 D. of this when he is at school-work, 2 D. of this remainder he requires to correct his hyperopia, and so only 4 D. is left him for accommodation for near work. Hence he can read with his book 25 cms. distant without producing strain, but if he brings it nearer than this, he runs the risk of eyestrain. Lastly, as we have seen (page 70), the excessive use of accommodation over convergence is a fertile source of asthenopia.

With advancing years, the latent hyperopia becomes gradually (and finally, about the age of 40, entirely) manifest, and with diminution of accommodation range, the hyperope necessarily becomes prematurely "presbyopic." As we should expect, symptoms of eyestrain are much more common in presbyopes who are hyperopic, than in those who are emmetropic or myopic.

One of the results of *eyestrain* in young hyperopes, or in those who have to make great efforts to see small objects, as watchmakers, &c., is *spasm of the ciliary muscle*, whereby vision is accommodated to near objects, and the patient rendered myopic. This spasm "is usually accompanied by contracted pupil from associated spasm of the sphincter of the iris, both conditions being caused by direct or indirect irritation of the third nerve."[1]

According to Day,[2] "hypermetropic headache" is often accompanied by twitchings of the eyelids.

---

[1] Ross, "Nervous System," 1883, vol. i., p. 452.
[2] *Op. cit.*, p. 219.

Treatment of Hyperopia.—Having thoroughly tested the patient's eyes according to the plans enumerated on page 43, we proceed to give him correcting glasses.

We must bear in mind that, as the accommodation is never so relaxed as when it is under a mydriatic, we must forbear to give the full atropine correction. Donders suggests that it is a good rule to neutralise the whole of the Hm and $\frac{1}{4}$ of the Hl. Thus a patient with Ht = 2.5 D., of which .5 D. is manifest, and consequently 2 D. latent, should have as glasses to wear always $+$ 1 D. *i.e.*, .5 $+ \frac{1}{4} \times$ 2.

<small>Landolt says, "The convex glass ought to correct the whole of the refractive defect, and, moreover, disengage a certain amount (quota) of accommodation, which will help the person to keep up his ocular work the desired length of time."[1] He says that we should consider static and dynamic refraction as one whole. He would give a patient with hyperopia 9 D. and amplitude of accommodation 7 D., for distance $+$4 D., *i.e.*, his refraction deficit for distance, $+$ 2 D. added to one-third of his accommodative power ⁋, say 2 D., and for near work, say at 28 cms., he would give $+$ 8 D., calculated thus : to see at 28 cms. he requires $\frac{100}{28}$ =3.5 D. accommodative power added to his hyperopia 9 D. making 12.5 D., of this he can furnish 7 D., but if a glass 5.5 is given him, he will be using the whole of his accommodative power, hence we deduct from 7, one-third for the quota in reserve, *i.e.*, 7 - 2.5 = 4.5, that is, he can only supply 4.5 accommodation power for continuous work if he wishes to avoid asthenopia, 12.5 — 4.5 = 8, we, therefore, give him glasses $+$ 8 D. to work at 28 cms. with.</small>

Most surgeons prefer to follow Donders' plan, that is correct the whole of the manifest and one-quarter of the latent hyperopia, and order the glasses for constant use.

As a matter of fact, the ideal treatment would be to correct the *whole* of the hyperopia, because we thus render our patient emmetropic, and restore the harmony between the accommodation and convergence, and many surgeons when the patient is young, and the hyperopia moderate, say 4 or 5 dioptres, follow this plan. It has been my invariable

---

Op. cit., p. 378.

rule in such cases, to give the whole correction after deducting 1 D. for the atropine, and the results have been perfectly satisfactory. Of course, at first, the patient is sure to complain of the glasses, but, by the rigid use of them, taking care that they shall be circular, so that he cannot look over them, the eyes will soon conform to the altered conditions, and the patient will probably return in a couple of months perfectly satisfied.

This plan when adopted with those that have developed internal strabismus has often the happiest results, for we may cure the squint without resorting to an operation.

Lang and Barrett have shown, that the spectacle treatment completely and rapidly cures 10 per cent. of convergent strabismus, and as long as the glass is worn 33 per cent., and the effect is in direct ratio to the youth of the patients.[1] Moreover, these are the hyperopes who can most readily be made practically "emmetropic" and therefore get the greatest gain from the glasses; for their very defect, the squint, shows that they have been unable to dissociate their accommodation and convergence. It is this habit of using their accommodation in excess, which prevents many hyperopes from taking full correction. They cannot unlearn the habit, and naturally the older the patient the more probability is there of this being the case. In such cases we must commence with a much weaker convex glass, and we must hope to be able to increase it later. We must treat every case on its own merits; when the amplitude of accommodation is great, the patient will probably prefer a weaker glass than we wish to give, and *vice versâ*. When the hyperopia is slight, the vision good, and no symptoms of strain are present, we should abstain from ordering any glass.

---

[1] *R. L. O. H. Reports*, vol. xii., p. 15.

It is important to remember that hyperopia tends to decrease towards emmetropia. A child may be hyperopic to the extent of 2 D., and as the growth and development of the different parts of the body proceed, the flatness of the eye may disappear, and by puberty it may be emmetropic. For this reason it may be necessary to re-examine the eyes of children almost every second year, in order to make quite sure they are not wearing a too strong convex glass, which would induce an artificial myopia, which in turn might lead to real myopia.

As a last word I cannot do better than quote the excellent advice given by Day when writing on the subject of "Hypermetropic Headache." He says, "Hypermetropia is often aggravated by objection to spectacles, due, not only to vanity, but to the erroneous opinion that glasses weaken the sight. The patient must be imperatively urged to consult an experienced oculist, else, dreading the horrors of waiting-rooms, consulting-rooms, and ophthalmoscopes, he is apt to seek the aid of a spectacle-maker, who is never to be depended upon, for the condition known as latent hypermetropia has to be taken into account, especially in those cases where headache is the most prominent symptom, and latent hypermetropia cannot be tested except by the aid of mydriatics and other measures which must be left entirely in the hands of a qualified oculist."[1]

Illustrative cases. *Ciliary Asthenopia—Hyperopia.*

A. E., aged 14, a healthy school boy suffers from slight conjunctivitis and blepharitis, and complains that in the evening after "preparation" his eyes and head always ache. He takes the usual amount of outdoor exercise that English boys are accustomed to.

He has no squint and $\genfrac{}{}{0pt}{}{R\ V}{L\ V}\} = \frac{6}{6} + 1\ D. = \frac{6}{6}\ P = 12\ cms. \therefore p = \frac{100}{12\frac{1}{2}} = 8\ D.$

---

[1] *Op. cit.*, p. 219.

Under atropine, keratoscopy reveals hyperopia in both eyes to the extent of 3 D.

$$a = 8+3 = 11 \text{ D.}$$

He has been able to dissociate his accommodation from his convergence efforts and thus avoided squint, and his asthenopia is due to the excessive use of accommodation over convergence.

He was given convex glasses 1.5 D. for both eyes for constant use, which in a short time effectually removed his troubles.

Asthenopia from Abuse—Spasm of Accommodation—Slight Hyperopia.

F. M., 25, seamstress. Her work is very fine embroidery. She complains after work of pain in the eyes and brow, and very often lately the pain comes on during work.

$$\begin{matrix} R V < \frac{6}{12} \\ L V < \frac{6}{9} \end{matrix} > -.5D = \frac{6}{6}$$

Under homatropine, the shadow test shows that she is very slightly hyperopic, viz., $+.5$ D. in both eyes.

She was given glasses $+1$ D. to wear at her work.

XI. **ASTIGMATISM** (Ἀ privative, στίγμα a point) as its name implies, is a condition of the eye in which the rays passing through, do not all focus at one point, we have:

(1) *Irregular Astigmatism:* this is due to a difference of refraction in different parts of the same meridian. It is produced by various causes, among them being, a difference in the refractive power of the several sectors of the lens; changes, or displacements of the lens; and changes in the cornea, such as nebulæ.

(2) *Regular Astigmatism:* this is due to a difference of refraction in different meridians of the eye, the maximum and minimum being at right angles to each other. Parallel rays passing through a convex spherical lens unite at a point, the principle focus, if the curvatures of the lens are all uniform; but if this is not the case, if for instance, the vertical curvature is greater than the horizontal, the rays passing through the former, will unite sooner than those passing through the latter. This is what we find in regular astigmatism. If the curvature of the horizontal

meridian of the eye is such, that the rays passing through it focus on the retina, and that of the vertical meridian is greater, and the rays passing through it focus in front of the retina, we have simple myopic astigmatism.

Every eye is astigmatic to a certain extent, but the degree of astigmatism is very little, and " so long as astigmatism does not essentially diminish the acuteness of vision, we call it normal " (Donders).

The Seat of Astigmatism is mostly in the *cornea*, due either to congenital malformation, or to acquired alteration of the curves, the result of operations, etc., but it is also found in the lens, and is then the inverse of that of the cornea, and is due to an *un-equal contraction of the ciliary muscle*, causing the lens to become more convex in one meridian, and thus more or less counteracting the effect of the corneal astigmatism (Dobrowolsky).

Donders says, " with a high degree of asymmetry of the cornea asymmetry of the crystalline lens exists, acting in such a direction, that the astigmatism for the whole eye is nearly always less than that proceeding from the cornea." [1]

As the result of an examination with Javal's ophthalmometer, of the eyes of 226 scholars between the ages of 7 and 20, Nordenson says, that corneal astigmatism equal to at least one and a half dioptres is quite compatible, in young people, with normal acuity of vision, and that a correction of the corneal astigmatism by means of the lens is in them the general rule.[2]

The following table shows the different varieties of regular astigmatism :—

---

[1] *Op. cit.*, p. 492.
[2] *Oph. Rev.*, vol. 2, p. 205.

Variety of Astigmatism.	Refraction of the Principal Meridians.	Position of the Principal Focus.

i. HYPEROPIC ASTIGMATISM.
    a. Simple   { Emmetropic ....on the retina.
                           { Hyperopic ....behind the retina.
    b. Compound   Both hyperopic......both behind the retina, one being nearer than the other.

ii. MYOPIC ASTIGMATISM.
    a. Simple   { Emmetropic ....on the retina.
                           { Myopic ....in front of the retina.
    b. Compound   Both myopic ....both in front of the retina, one nearer than the other.

iii. MIXED ASTIGMATISM { Hyperopic ....behind the retina.
                                  { Myopic ....in front of the retina.

Hyperopic astigmatism occurs more frequently than any other form; next in order is myopic astigmatism; and mixed astigmatism is the rarest. In my own experience I find that out of 2,316 refraction cases—

    326 suffered from hyperopic astigmatism;
    260   „   myopic astigmatism; and
    36   „   mixed astigmatism.

Donders says, "Most cases of abnormal astigmatism belong to the hypermetropic form."[1]

The vertical meridian, or one near it, is generally the most convex (Landolt). This is called "astigmatism according to the rule." Thus, in hyperopic astigmatism, the horizontal meridian is hyperopic in Simple and Mixed As., and the most hyperopic in Comp. As. and in myopic astigmatism, *vice versâ;* when the reverse occurs, it is called "astigmatism against the rule." Examining the notes of all the cases of astigmatism (of which I have kept an accurate record of the direction and refraction of the meridians), I find that out of 1,126 eyes, 812

---

[1] *Op. cit.*, p. 520.

(*i.e.*, 72 per cent.) are "according to the rule," viz., with the horizontal meridian most hyperopic, or the vertical meridian most myopic. They are classified as follows:—

"According to the Rule."		"Against the Rule."	Meridian at an Angle of 40°, 45° or 50°.[1]
H. As.	458	82	
M. As.	300	128	98
Mixed As.	54	6	
	812	216	98

We see from the above that hyperopic astigmatism "according to the rule" is more than five times more frequent than "against the rule," whereas in myopic astigmatism, it is only a little more than twice as frequent.

Diagnosis and Symptoms of Astigmatism.—The acuteness of vision is below the normal. Spherical glasses may improve the distant sight to a certain extent, but the correction is never complete. On directing the patient to look with one eye at Snellen's "Fan," placed five or six metres off, or nearer if necessary, we find that he can see certain lines more distinctly than others. The vertical lines may be seen quite black and distinct, the horizontal lines being faint, or *vice versâ;* or the oblique lines on one side may be distinct, those on the other side, at right angles to the former, being indistinct. If all the radiating lines are indistinct, we must make one of the meridians emmetropic, by placing up before the eye the weakest concave or strongest convex spherical glass, that is required to make one set of lines distinct and black.

When rays coming from a point are refracted at an astigmatic surface, a linear image of the point is formed at the

---

[1] Oblique meridians of less than 40° from the horizontal or vertical are reckoned as horizontal or vertical.

focus of each principal meridian; and the direction of the linear image *is at right angles* to the meridian at whose focus it is formed (Frost).

Thus, if a patient sees the horizontal lines distinctly, and the lines as they pass to the vertical become less distinct, reaching the maximum of indistinctness in the vertical lines, we know that the *vertical meridian* is emmetropic, or nearly so. Such a patient would complain that the letters of the test type were spread out horizontally, and if we place before the eye, in a frame, a stenopaic disc, with the slit vertical, we shall find all his symptoms of astigmatism disappear. He sees all the lines with equal clearness, and the letters appear normal, because the vertical slit has cut off all the horizontal rays that caused the blurring. The best method for diagnosing astigmatism is the "*Shadow Test.*" By this method we not only detect the presence of astigmatism, which we have often failed to discover by other means, such as the "Fan" and the stenopaic disc; but we also determine accurately the amount of ametropia in each meridian, and the direction of the principal meridians, and this is all done with a speed and certainty that renders it the greatest boon to the surgeon. Of course it is very important, whenever it can be done, for the patient's eyes to be under the influence of a mydriatic.

The *degree of astigmatism* is the difference between the refractions of the two principal meridians.

One of the most important symptoms of astigmatism is *asthenopia*. The American table (fig. 1) on page 28 shows that in hyperopic astigmatism 50 per cent. were asthenopic, in myopic astigmatism 72 per cent., and in mixed astigmatism 74 per cent. My table (fig. 2), on page 29, shows that in hyperopic astigmatism 28 per cent. were asthenopic, and in myopic astigmatism 41 per cent.

Marlow says that headache is a very common symptom of astigmatism; he says the tendency to headache in ametropes reaches its highest point in compound hyperopic astigmatism, 85 per cent. of the cases suffering from headache. He further says, "Although astigmatism of this low degree" (.25 D.) "has rarely much influence upon visual acuteness, its power to produce *troublesome asthenopia and headaches* of the severest kind is, I believe, great, and underestimated by many ophthalmologists."[1] Chisolm says that with acute vision, headache after eye use, usually indicates the presence of astigmatism of low degree, and the lesser degree causes the severer headache.[2] He reports that during one year he prescribed 600 pairs of glasses of only .25 D. of astigmatism. All these patients suffered from headache, eye pains and other symptoms of asthenopia, and the majority of them were cured by this treatment.[3] But as a general rule, even .5 D. of astigmatism does not call for correction by any such marked symptoms of asthenopia. Savage, of New York, says that astigmatism causes least inconvenience when the principal meridians are, for both eyes, horizontal and vertical; more when they are oblique but symmetrical, and most when oblique but homonomous.[4] One of Donders' patients, a man, aged 26, records his asthenopic symptoms in a very graphic manner, thus:—

"My occupation is that of a clerk. The first effort to work was the most painful. Thereupon dazzling soon followed, obliging me to shut my eyes, and to keep them closed for some time. After that my work went on somewhat better, but I found it impossible to work all the forenoon; I was constantly obliged to leave off. At the end my

---

[1] *Oph. Rev.*, vol. viii., p. 359.
[2] *Oph. Rev.*, vol x., p. 280.
[3] "International Clinics," vol. i., p. 328.
[4] *Oph. Rev.*, vol. vi., p. 245.

eyes were painful, and I felt best when I walked for a considerable time in the open air, out of the sun. In the evening, by gaslight, my work went on at first pretty well, but soon red dazzling came on. I was then obliged every time to leave off, and with fatigued and painful eyes I returned home." [1]

He was suffering from simple hyperopic astigmatism, the horizontal meridian being hyperopic to the extent of 2 D., and the vertical meridian emmetropic. The correction of the astigmatism by cylindrical glasses + 2 D., with the axis vertical, removed all his symptoms of asthenopia.

The causes of accomodative asthenopia in astigmatism are:—

(1) *The confusion of the images* and the attempts made by the ciliary muscle to remove it.

Brailey says, in referring to astigmatic asthenopia, " From this frequently varying accommodative effort, fatigue and aching of the eyes often result. Or even if the ciliary muscle be powerful enough to prevent fatigue, and to perform its best for the correction of the astigmatism, the *confusion of the images* and the consequent mental condition are sufficient to cause severe headaches."[2]

This confusion is worse in hyperopic astigmatism. We have seen that the curvature of the vertical meridian is always the greatest in astigmatism " according to the rule," hence the letters are spread out laterally and the words appear very confused; we can prove this for ourselves by holding up before one eye (the other being closed) a concave cylinder of, say, 1.5 D., with its axis vertical; if we turn the axis round to the horizontal, making ourselves vertically hyperopic, the letters are spread out vertically and the words are very much clearer.

---

[1] *Op. cit.*, page 521.
[2] *Guy's Hosp. Rep.*, 1878, p. 3.

(2) *Meridional asymmetrical accommodation*, or unequal contraction of the ciliary muscle. Fick asserts that this is the cause of asthenopia in many astigmatics,[1] and is due to the effort to compensate for the astigmatism of the cornea by producing an artificial astigmatism of the lens, which is the inverse of that of the cornea (see page 80).

Martin considers that the *partial contraction* of the ciliary muscle, which he says takes place in astigmatism, is a very common cause of megrim, and he says that when the headache is unilateral, it is on the same side as the eye in which this partial contraction is taking place.[2]

(3) *Hyperopia.*—In simple hyperopic astigmatism we have seen that when the astigmatism is "according to the rule," the horizontal meridian is hyperopic, and the vertical emmetropic. If a person with this defect corrects his horizontal meridian, he must at the same time, make his vertical meridian myopic (unless, according to Dobrowolsky and Fick, he has acquired the power of contracting his ciliary muscle unequally). Now he can get rid of this confusing vertical meridian by partially closing his eyes, which has more or less the same effect as a horizontal stenopaic slit; he then virtually makes himself a simple hyperope, and will suffer from asthenopia under the same conditions as a hyperope.

In compound hyperopic astigmatism the same occurs. The horizontal meridian is most hyperopic if the astigmatism is "according to the rule," and here then we must expect, all the more, to get strain; and so also in mixed astigmatism.

Remembering that hyperopic astigmatism is by far the

---

[1] *Knapp's Arch. of Oph.*, xviii., p. 321.
[2] *Annales d'Oculistique*, 1888, i., p. 122.

commonest form of the defect, there is no doubt that a very fruitful cause of astigmatic asthenopia is hyperopia, which takes us back to the statement made by Donders, "That in the pure form of asthenopia hypermetropia is scarcely ever wanting."[1]

Treatment of Astigmatism.—Cylindrical lenses are lenses ground, as if cut from the surface of a cylinder, convex cylindrical lenses from the external surface of a solid cylinder, and concave cylindrical lenses from the inner surface of a hollow cylinder. These lenses have the property of only acting on rays that pass at right angles to their axis, and hence by their means we can very accurately correct regular astigmatism.

Having ascertained by the "shadow test," or any other method, the refraction of the two principal meridians, we confirm this by testing the patient with combinations of glasses before the test types. For instance, suppose we find that the patient is hyperopic to the extent of 5 D. in the horizontal, and 3 D. in the vertical meridian. The difference between these gives the amount of astigmatism, viz., 2 D., therefore we choose a cylinder + 2 D., and the direction of its axis is at right angles to the meridian of greatest refraction; in this case it must be placed in the frame vertically. In front of this cylinder we put a + 3 D. spherical glass. We shall have then corrected his astigmatism, for the rays passing through the horizontal plane are passing through a lens of + 5 D., thus correcting the horizontal hyperopia of 5 D., and those passing through the vertical plane are uninfluenced by the cylinder because they are passing through its axis, and are only influenced by the spherical glass + 3 D., which corrects the vertical hyperopia of 3 D.

---

[1] *Op. cit.*, p. 261.

If the patient was under atropine during the examination, we take off + 1 D. from the convex spherical lens, and in myopic astigmatism we add the same amount, but this is no fixed rule; some surgeons give the whole atropine correction to young subjects. In adults, when they have recovered from the atropine, it is always best to subject them to a confirmatory examination before the test types, for some slight alteration in the spherical glass may be great improvement.

When fitting the patient with cylinders, it should be our aim to strictly adhere to the degree and direction of the astigmatism, ascertained under atropine, although the patient may prefer some alteration, owing probably to the partial contraction of the ciliary muscle, which we have seen is a cause of asthenopia, and which consequently we wish to remove.

We must not always expect to get normal acuteness of vision at first, but after the glasses have been worn for a time we often find great improvement. In ordering the glasses, care must be taken to indicate accurately the axis of the cylinder. Unfortunately there is at present no uniformity as to the numbering of the degrees on the trial frames and optician's order forms. I have before me now three forms issued by different opticians, and they all differ. The simplest way is to indicate the number of degrees from the vertical or horizontal thus :—

In mixed astigmatism we may choose either a concave cylinder in one direction, or a convex cylinder in the other.

The glasses correcting the astigmatism should be worn constantly. If, associated with the cylinders, the patient requires spherical glasses to correct hyperopia, myopia, or presbyopia, such glasses should be ordered according to the plane already described.

XII. **ANISOMETROPIA.**—("A, privative, ἴσος, equal, μέτρον, measure, ὤψ, eye) is a condition in which the refraction of the two eyes is different.

Every possible combination may exist. When one eye is astigmatic and the other hyperopic or myopic, the astigmatic eye has generally the same form of ametropia as the non-astigmatic eye.

Except when it is the consequence of an operation, loss of lens, &c., anisometropia may be regarded as *congenital*, and attributable to the unequal development of the eyes (Landolt). The difference in the refraction of the two eyes may be very great—I have seen a difference of ten dioptres.

If we except cases showing only a difference of half a dioptre between the two eyes, anisometropia is not common. It is chiefly met with in astigmatism. It has been suggested, that when the refraction of the eyes is different in kind, *i.e.*, when one eye is hyperopic and the other is myopic or emmetropic, the term antimetropia should be used, but it has not been universally adopted.

There are *three varieties of anisometropia* :—

1. Simultaneous binocular vision exists.
2. The eyes are used alternately.
3. One of the eyes is permanently excluded.

1. *Simultaneous binocular vision.*—We must first prove that binocular vision exists. This we can do by means of a prism, base up before one eye, or better still, by means of *Snellen's coloured glasses.*

When at Utrecht in 1880 I was particularly struck by the ease and certainty with which this apparatus revealed the non-use of one eye, and, with Professor Snellen's permission, I introduced it at Moorfields. It is now so well known that a full description is hardly necessary. It consists of a frame, hung up before the window, in which letters of coloured glass, alternately green and red, are placed. The patient, standing in front of them at four or five metres distance, is provided with a spectacle frame into which one red and one green glass is placed, the colour of these glasses being of the same intensity as that of the letters. Only the red letters can be seen through the red glass, and the green letters through the green glass, so that each eye separately only sees half the letters. The letters in the frame may be made to spell a word, such as F R I E N D, and so arranged that the letters F, I and N are red, and R, E and D green. If the patient, having had any ametropia corrected, sees all the letters and spells the word "friend" we know he has binocular vision, but if, e.g., he only spells F I N, we know that he is using the eye with the red glass in front of it, and that the other eye is excluded from vision. The chief value of this test is that there can be no deception—a person may know that he has to see double with a prism, and assert that he does, but I have never known Snellen's apparatus fail.

For binocular vision to exist in anisometropia the difference in refraction between the two eyes—that is, the degree of anisometropia—must be small, although cases have been recorded where it has amounted to 6 D., or even more. Landolt refers to a patient of his, who was emmetropic with the right eye and hyperopic by 3 D. in the left, and who, nevertheless, had perfect binocular vision. Under these circumstances, although the magnitude and acuteness of the images on the two retinas are unequal, they overlap and help each other.

If each ciliary muscle could act independently, the anisometrope could very often correct each eye by a separate and independent accommodation in each eye, but it is generally believed that the same effort of accommodation is made on both sides, with the result that on one retina the image is sharp, while on the other it is diffused.

Fick, of Zurich,[1] says that unequal accommodation in the two eyes simultaneously *is* possible, producing (1), an

---

[1] *Knapp's Arch. of Oph.*, vol. xviii., p. 292.

unequal effect in both eyes if the refraction of both is the same, or (2) an equal effect in both eyes if anisometropia exists. He considers as proofs of this that, despite extensive anisometropia, binocular vision may be present, and that complete correction of the anisometropia, by lenses of different foci, is not well tolerated in a majority of cases, but that the patient feels more comfortable with lenses of nearly the same strength; and further, that physiologically within certain limits, the accommodation of one eye can act independently of that of its partner. On the other hand Hess criticises Fick's experiments, and maintains that Hering, Donders and Rumpf were right, and that unsymmetrical accommodative effort is impossible.[1] Fick says that this unequal accommodation is very limited, and can only be obtained by a perceptible and sometimes a painful exertion. This explains the asthenopia, and also the fact that the strain is more often present in those whose anisometropia is of a low degree. Any one can make the experiment for himself. If, say, an anisometropia of 1 D. be made by putting up +.5 in front of one eye, and −.5 in front of the other, and the page of a book read, the feeling of strain is much more marked than when 3 D. of anisometropia is made by putting up +1.5 and −1.5 in front of the eyes. The opponents of Fick's theory maintain that it is not the actual unequal accommodation, but the futile attempts to make it, that causes the asthenopia.

(2) The eyes are used alternately. One eye may be emmetropic or slightly hyperopic, and is used for distance, and the other eye is myopic and is used for near work.

(3) One eye is permanently excluded. If the inequality is very great, the best eye is used exclusively, vision is ignored with the other eye, which becomes amblyopic, and deviates inwards, or more commonly outwards.

---

[1] *Graefe, Arch. f. Oph.*, bd. 35, i., p. 157.

In these two last varieties of anisometropia, if asthenopia is present it is caused by the ametropia only, and not by the anisometropia.

Treatment of Anisometropia.—When binocular vision exists, the treatment varies considerably; we should expect that each eye should be fitted with its correcting glass in all cases, but in practice we find this will not suit many patients—they have become so accustomed to the difference in each eye that the removal of the difference not only confers no benefit, but proves irksome, and they may complain of dazzling, head-swimming and headache. The rule to adopt is the following: If the ametropia is of a low degree, and binocular vision acute and easy at any distance, without glasses, and there is no asthenopia, then we leave the patient alone; if there *is* asthenopia, we try giving similar glasses for both eyes, the glass to be selected by trial. We find generally that the glass is weaker than that required by the most ametropic eye; for instance, suppose the right eye is emmetropic and the left hyperopic to the extent of $+\ 2$ D., glasses of $+\ 1$ D. for both eyes may suit best, if not, then perhaps the patient bears best a full correction of the ametropic eye, and a plain glass in front of the emmetropic one. Full correction for each eye should be our aim, and we must get as near to it as we can, the patient's sensations, after full trial, being our guide.

In the young, it is advisable to give full correction for each eye, and order the glasses to be circular and worn always.

When binocular vision does not exist, but each eye is used, one for distance and the other for reading, if asthenopia is not present, the patient will not thank you to give him any glasses. Although he has lost binocular vision he has gained other advantages; in some cases he can entirely dispense with muscular effort, his ciliary muscle and internal recti being rarely used.

When asthenopia exists, we shall find probably that both eyes are ametropic, one more so than the other, and glasses are needed. The best plan is to give similar glasses for both eyes. If both eyes are hyperopic, we give the glasses corresponding to the strongest hyperopic eye; this latter eye will then be used for distance and the other one for near work. If both eyes are myopic, we give each the correcting glass of the weaker; when one eye only is used, this should be corrected according to the principles laid down, and the other eye, if not diseased, should be corrected, and the correcting glass put in a spectacle frame with ground glass before the better eye, and the patient should be made to practise with these glasses for a certain time every day, and if there is any improvement the question of an operation for strabismus will arise. This eye can never be expected to take its place in binocular vision, but in some cases it may become very useful, especially if any damage or disease should affect the good eye, and moreover, the cosmetic result which sometimes occurs is a great benefit.

Illustrative cases: Accommodative Asthenopia, Hyperopic Astigmatism, Anisometropia.

Miss G., aged 19, student, enjoys good health, accustomed to read and do needlework many hours a day. Complains of pain in eyes and in the middle of the forehead coming on after close work—in fact, she can do very little needlework without fatigue and pain. The night's rest removes all the symptoms.

Examination.— R.V. = $\frac{9}{9}$.
L.V. = $\frac{6}{15}$.

Maddox test reveals ½ metre angle of latent convergence, for distance. Under *atropine*, "Shadow test" shows—

R. $\underset{+3}{+\!\!\!\!\!\!\!+}\,+4$ L. $\underset{+2}{+\!\!\!\!\!\!\!+}\,+4$

She was ordered glasses as follows for constant use :—
$$R. + 1 \text{ D. cyl. axis vertical.}$$
$$L. + 2.5 \text{ D. cyl. axis vertical.}$$

The fatigue was caused evidently by the (1) unequal accommodation, the result of the astigmatism and the anisometropia, and (2) the hyperopia.

She was seen again after three months, and most of her symptoms had disappeared, her vision being $\frac{6}{9}$ with both eyes.

Asthenopia, Anisometropia, Astigmatism.

S. F., aged 14, a healthy girl, complains of her eyes and head aching, and everything becoming confused after reading or working for a short time.

$$\text{Under atropine V.} = \begin{cases} R. \ \frac{6}{9} \ \bar{c} \ - \ 7.5 \text{ D. sph.} \\ \qquad - \ 1 \text{ D. cyl. axis horiz.} = \frac{6}{15} \\ L. \ \frac{6}{18} \ \bar{c} \ + \ .5 \text{ D. sph.} \\ \qquad + \ .5 \text{ D. cyl. axis vertical} = \frac{6}{9} \end{cases}$$

Full correction was ordered for right eye and the cylinder for left, for *constant use*. She returned later with the asthenopic symptoms almost gone.

G. P., aged 33, compositor, suffers from chronic blepharitis, granular lids, &c.

$$R. \ \tfrac{6}{9} \ \bar{c} \ - \ .5 \text{ D. cyl. axis vertical} = \tfrac{6}{6}$$
$$L. \ \tfrac{6}{60} \ \bar{c} \ + \ 4 \text{ D. sph.}$$
$$\qquad + \ 1 \text{ D. cyl. axis horiz.} = \tfrac{6}{18}$$

Glasses ordered. Recovery complete.

Asthenopia—Anisometropia.

Mr. K., aged 53, complains of pain in the eyes and forehead after reading. He has never worn glasses, and always finds a great relief by covering up his right eye when reading. He has binocular vision.

$$V. = \begin{cases} R. \ \tfrac{6}{9} \text{ no improvement.} \\ L. \ \tfrac{6}{15} - 1 = \tfrac{6}{9} \end{cases}$$

R.E. $\bar{c} + 2$ D. $P = 25$ cms. $\therefore a = 4 - 2 - 0 = 2$
L.E. $\qquad P = 33$ cms. $\therefore a = 3 - 1 = 2$..

He had evidently used his right eye for distance and his left for reading. He was tried with several combinations, and preferred $+ 1.5$ D. for both eyes. These were given to him for reading.

PART III.

MUSCULAR ASTHENOPIA.

MUSCULAR ASTHENOPIA.

I. ANATOMICAL AND PHYSIOLOGICAL CONSIDERATIONS.—The eyeball lies in the orbital socket, surrounded by Tenon's capsule, which is the thickened anterior layer of the cellular tissue of the orbit. The muscles which move the eye are six in number, and with the exception of the inferior oblique, which arises from the anterior and inner part of the floor of the orbit, they all arise from the apex of the orbit. These muscles may be considered as three pairs—each pair rotating the eye round a particular axis. The four recti—viz., superior, inferior, internal and external—pass forwards, pierce Tenon's capsule, from which they receive a sheath, become tendinous, and are inserted into the sclerotic not far from the margin of the cornea, the most anterior insertion being that of the internal rectus, which is about six mm. from the margin of the cornea. The superior oblique passes forwards to the upper and inner angle of the orbit, then it becomes temporarily tendinous and passes through a pulley, after which it becomes muscular again, and changes its direction, passing backwards and outwards through Tenon's capsule to be inserted (tendinously) into the sclerotic, at the back and upper part of the eye. The inferior oblique passes outwards and backwards underneath the inferior rectus, and then between the external rectus and the eye, to be inserted in the outer, posterior and lower part of the eyeball, not very far from the entrance of the optic nerve.

The axis of rotation of the internal and external recti is vertical, that of the superior and inferior recti, horizontal, with the inner extremity more forward than the outer (fig. 9), and that of the oblique muscles lies also in the horizontal plane, with its anterior extremity tilted outwards.[1]

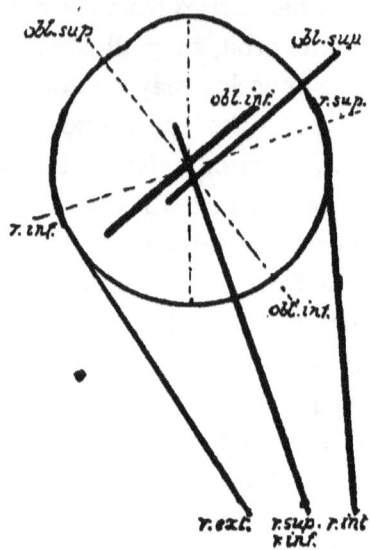

FIG. 9.

Diagram of the attachments of the muscles of the eye and of their axes of rotation (the latter being represented by dotted lines). The axis of rotation of the internal and external rectus, being perpendicular to the plane of the paper, is not represented.

The movement of looking—

1. Upwards is produced by { Superior rectus.
                            { Inferior oblique.

2. Downwards   ,,   ,, { Inferior rectus.
                             { Superior oblique.

3. Outwards   ,,   ,, External rectus.

4. Inwards   ,,   ,, Internal rectus.

---

[1] "Text-book of Physiology" (Michael Foster), 5th edition, p. 1284.

ANATOMICAL AND PHYSIOLOGICAL CONSIDERATIONS. 99

When both eyes look to the right we have contraction of the right external and left internal recti, and when they look to left, the left external and right internal recti.

Movement of the eyes, up and in, is produced by 1 and

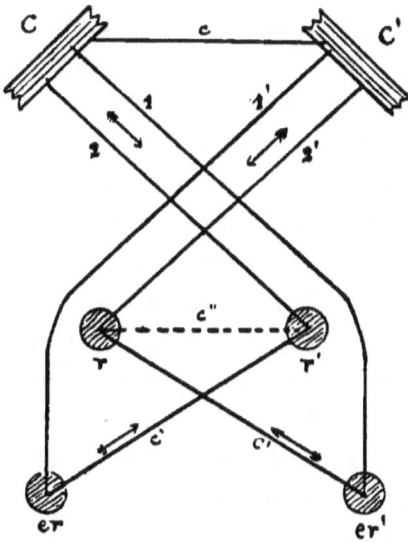

FIG. 10 (after Ross).

C C′, cortex of right and left cerebral hemispheres. 1, 2, fibres of the pyramidal tract uniting C, the cortex of the right hemisphere, and r′ and er′, the nuclei of the *left* internal and external rectus. 1′, 2′, fibres of the pyramidal tract connecting the cortex of the left hemisphere with r and er, the nuclei of the *right* internal and external rectus muscles. c, fibres of the corpus callosum, uniting identical regions of the two hemispheres. c′, commissural fibres, connecting the spinal nucleus of the internal rectus of one eye with that of the external rectus of the opposite eye; c″, suggested commissural fibres connecting the nuclei of the two internal recti.

4, viz., superior rectus, inferior oblique, and internal rectus; movement down and out, by 2 and 3, and so on.

The external rectus is supplied by the sixth nerve, the superior oblique by the fourth, and the remainder by the third.

Convergence of the eyes is produced by the associated movements of both the internal recti. The nuclei (r r′ fig.

10), of that part of the third nerve that supplies these muscles may be connected by fibres (c″), carrying out the principle that there is bilateral association of the nerve nuclei of muscles bilaterally associated in their action (Broadbent). This explains the convergence of a covered eye.

A. Graefe says that one of the factors that cause the covered eye to converge is a "Convergenzgefühl," or as Hansen Grut expresses it, a "Nahebewusstsein"—a consciousness of nearness. Landolt denies this, and asserts that the excluded eye fixes correctly through the connection between accommodation and convergence alone. It is important to remember that when a stimulus passes primarily to the nucleus of the internal rectus, it is associated with the same muscle of the opposite side and convergence takes place; whereas the conjugate movements of the eyes to the right or left, are produced by stimuli passing *primarily* to the nucleus of the *external* rectus, which nucleus is connected with the nucleus of the internal rectus of the opposite side (fig. 10). We may have both these stimuli occurring at the same time, viz., primary stimulus to the internal recti to converge, and to the external rectus of one side associated with the internal rectus of the other side, to produce lateral movements of the eyes.

A very good proof that these two actions are separate, is found in a case reported by Millikin of "Complete paralysis of the lateral movements of both eyes—ability to converge remaining intact."[1] The paralysis followed an attack of "grippe," and under iodide of potassium quite disappeared. There was no other nerve trouble except this inability of the eyes to move either to the right or the left. The lesion evidently affected the higher centre in the brain governing these movements. The convergence centre was intact.

And again, Stölting and Bruns[2] observed in a lady, aged 30, paralysis of convergence, while the associated movements of both eyes inwards remained intact.

---

[1] *American Journal of Ophthalmology*, vol. vii., p. 311.
[2] *Graefe, Arch.*, bd. xxxiv., 3, p. 92.

ANATOMICAL AND PHYSIOLOGICAL CONSIDERATIONS. 101

The nuclei of the third nerve are situated in the hind part of the floor of the third ventricle, and the front part of the floor of the aqueduct (Michael Foster), and are so associated that contraction of the ciliary muscles for accommodation, of the pupils, and of the internal recti for convergence, are all three associated in their actions. One impulse, viz., a psychical impression, a wish to look at a near object,

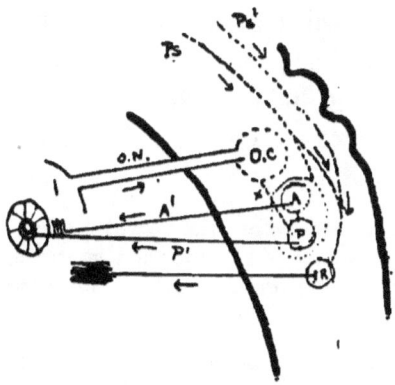

FIG. 11.

Scheme showing the oculo-motor centre and some of its connections (adapted from Erb).

Ps, psychical impression (the wish to accommodate being the stimulus). Ps', psychical impression for voluntary converging strabismus. A, accommodation centre, and P, centre for contractor fibres of iris, the two forming the oculo-motor centre. I R, internal rectus centre, with motor nerve to internal rectus muscle. P', motor nerve to constrictor of the pupil. A', motor nerve to ciliary muscle. O. N., optic nerve from retina to O. C, optic centre, and connected with P, the constrictor centre. X, is the seat of the lesion causing reflex pupillary immobility.

passes from the motor centre in the cortex of the brain to these nuclei, and the result of this one impulse is the united action of these different muscles; the action is not always simultaneous, for convergence often lags behind accommodation (see page 112).[1]

---

[1] See paper by Berry, *Trans. Oph. Soc.*, vol. xi., p. 156.

Fig. 11 shows diagrammatically the supposed position of the nuclei of the third nerve : A, the accommodation centre lies most anteriorly near the middle line; behind it, and further removed from the middle line lies P, the centre for the sphincter of the iris, and further back still IR, the nucleus of the internal rectus (Hensen and Voelckers; see also paper by Perlia in *Graefe, Arch.*, bd. xxxv., iv., p. 287):

Many people can voluntarily squint inwards, but when they do this, they will be found to accommodate for a near point at the same time; some few can, however, do so without accommodating, and in such cases the psychical impression probably passes straight to the nucleus of the internus by Ps' (fig. 11).

Bruce, in a paper read before the Royal Society of Edinburgh in 1889, hints at the existence of a pre-formed centre for the association of accommodation and convergence, which Berry truly says cannot be supported clinically.[1]

Man has binocular vision, that is, the image from an object falls upon the retina of both eyes simultaneously, and in normal binocular vision on exactly the same region of the retina, for if the images did not overlap, two images would be seen, and so-called "double vision" would be the result. The best and quickest test for determining whether binocular vision is present, or not, is Snellen's apparatus described on page 89.

It has been urged that Snellen's glasses are not a test of binocular single or "fusion" vision, but only, if one may use the term, of double monocular vision; but if the patient answers to the test, and at the same time, when the glasses are removed has no diplopia, binocular vision *must* be present.

Whereas, then, in discussing ciliary strain we considered the eye simply as an optical apparatus, now we must con-

---

[1] *Oph. Rev.*, vol. x., p. 26.

sider the two eyes together as forming *one whole*, and on their proper associated movements must depend perfect binocular vision.

If binocular vision be impossible, through some great defect of the optical apparatus or the muscles, no attempt will be made to produce it, and no strain will follow. On the other hand, apparently normal binocular vision may exist, but to produce the effect, a demand in excess of the power will be put upon a muscle or a set of muscles, and the result will be strain, either producing, or tending to produce, the symptoms of muscular asthenopia.

II. THE RELATION OF THE TWO EYES TO EACH OTHER IN NORMAL DISTANT VISION. Michael Foster says that the *primary position* of the eyes is "that which is assumed when, with the head erect and vertical, we look straight forwards to the distant horizon; the visual axes of the two eyes are then parallel to each other and to the median plane;"[1] that is, in ideal binocular distant vision, the eyes being at rest and all the muscles in equilibrium with respect to each other, *the visual axes are parallel*. Ophthalmologists differ as to the correctness of this statement.

Grut, in his Bowman Lecture, 1889,[2] brings many arguments forward to show that the anatomical position of rest of the two eyes is *divergence*, and that the condition of parallelism in the normal eye is the result of a constant convergence innervation. Loring says that the equilibrium of the recti is a moderate degree of *convergence*. Berry made a careful examination of the equilibrium of the recti muscles in 120 persons, in whom all conditions of refraction were

---

[1] "Text-book of Physiology," 5th edit., p. 1278.
[2] *Trans. Oph. Soc.*, vol. x., p. 1.

represented, and he found that in the normal eye "a large proportion had either perfect or practically perfect parallelism,"[1] *i.e.*, a deviation of not more than $\frac{1}{5}$ m.a. Maddox found that the natural position of equilibrium for the two eyes in distant vision is one of slight convergence of the visual axes.[2] Schiötz,[3] of Christiania, says that the parallel position of equilibrium for distance exists in all cases where the muscular relations are normal.

If Grut is right in assuming the anatomical position of rest to be divergence, then removal of the stimulus to convergence innervation by binocular vision, ought to produce in every eye, unless spasm is present, divergence. In other words, in all normal eyes there ought to be found *latent divergence.*

Test for latent deviation of the eyes for distance.—If a person with normal vision be directed to look at an object in the distance, and one eye be covered for twenty or thirty seconds, if there is any latent deviation it becomes (as a rule) manifest, and on removal of the hand there will be diplopia for a brief space of time, and the covered eye will have to move, in order to fuse the two images—in, if there was latent divergence, and out, if convergence. A more accurate method of conducting this test is to destroy the possibility of binocular vision, *i.e.*, fusion, by means of a prism with its base up placed before one eye, or better still, by the apparatus suggested by Maddox called the "glass rod test;" by this means we can, not only, at once detect concealed deviation, but we can measure the amount. For full description of the Maddox test see *Ophthalmic*

---

[1] *Trans. Oph. Soc.*, vol. xi., p. 160.
[2] *Oph. Rev.*, vol. v., p. 341.
[3] *Knapp's Arch.*, vol. xix., p. 177.

Review, vol ix., p. 129.[1] Before this test is applied, any refractive defect must be corrected. By making a large number of examinations by this method, we can easily prove the correctness of Berry's statement (supporting Michael Foster's), viz., that *for all practical purposes the visual axes of the two eyes in normal binocular vision are parallel.* So much for what is called the static equilibrium of the ocular muscles. Now we proceed to examine the dynamic condition, that is, the relation of the muscles in binocular near vision—in other words, during *convergence*.

III. **CONVERGENCE** is "the direction that the eyes must give to their lines of fixation, in order that they may be simultaneously directed toward the point of fixation."[2] When both eyes are fixing an object six metres (or more) distant they are parallel, and c (which represents convergence) $= \frac{1}{\infty} = 0$; when the eyes simultaneously fix an object one metre off in the median line, both internal recti contract and the eyes converge, convergence is then said to be 1 metre angle, c = 1 m.a. This metre angle is the unit of convergence; if the eyes converge to a point 50 cms. off, then $c = \frac{1}{\frac{1}{2}} = 2$ m.a., if 20 cms. off $c = \frac{1}{\frac{1}{5}} = 5$ m.a. If the object is three metres off $c = \frac{1}{3} = .33$ m.a. To Nagel belongs the credit of devising this method of measuring the amount of convergence. The metre-angle (or "meterwinkel,"[3] as he calls it) of convergence corresponds to the dioptre of accommodation. Thus, an emmetrope who is fixing binocularly a point 25 cms. off is using 4 dioptres of accommodation, and his amount of convergence is $\frac{1}{\frac{1}{4}} = 4$ metres angle.

---

[1] The apparatus connected with this test, and also the Maddox test for deviation at ¼ metre, can be obtained from Messrs. Curry & Paxton, 195, Great Portland Street, W.

[2] "The Refraction and Accommodation of the Eye" (Landolt), p. 185.

[3] *Graefe-Sæmisch: Handbuch der Augenheilkunde*, bd. vi., p. 479.

Amplitude of Convergence.—We use the same formula as that used in estimating the amplitude of accommodation, viz.:

$$\frac{1}{A} = \frac{1}{P} - \frac{1}{R}$$

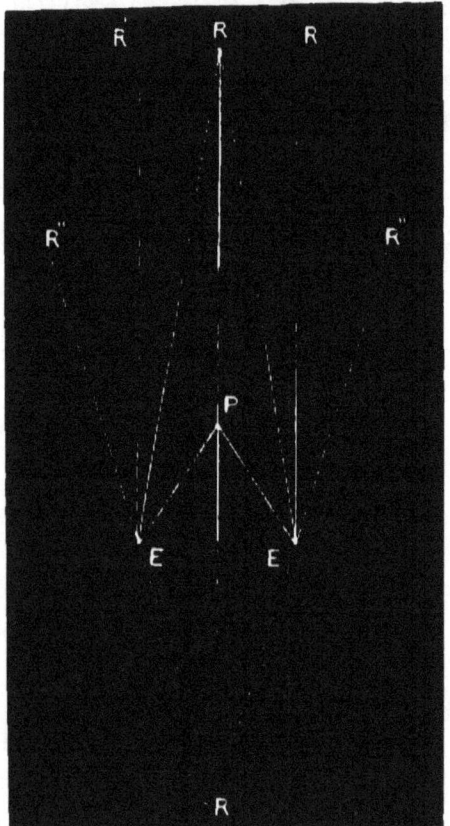

FIG. 12 (after Nagel and Landolt).

Where A is the amplitude or range of convergence, P is the punctum proximum, and R the punctum remotum of convergence. If we express the equation in metre angles, we have: "p" representing the maximum and "r" the minimum of convergence.

If R is at finite distance (fig. 12) we have $a = p - r$, that is, the amplitude of convergence is the amount of convergence required to direct the visual axes of the two eyes simultaneously to the point P, starting from the binocular distant point R. If R is at infinity, that is, if the visual axes are parallel (R', fig. 12), $R = \infty = 0$ and the equation stands—

$$a = p.$$

If the visual axes diverge, then R is beyond infinity (R", fig. 12) and the axes will meet at a point $- R$, which is negative; the equation will then be

$$a = p - (-r) = p + r.$$

To distinguish the equation from that used in accommodation it is common to prefix or affix a "c," thus:

$$ca = cp - cr,$$
$$\text{or} \quad a^c = p^c - r^c$$

The Punctum Remotum of Convergence.

Just as the punctum remotum of accommodation is the expression of the refraction *of the eye when completely at rest, so the punctum remotum of convergence is the expression of the* position *of the eyes when at rest—that is, when the impulse to fusion brought about by binocular vision is removed.* So that to find "R" we must find the *latent position* of the eyes for distance. This we do by the Maddox test, and the number of metre-angles read off on the scale gives us "r." If there is no latent deviation $r = 0$; if there is latent divergence "r" is negative, and if latent convergence it is positive.

According to Landolt and other writers, "r" is the expression of the minimum of convergence or the maximum of divergence, and is ascertained by the strongest prism, base in, that can be tolerated; the number of this prism divided by seven gives "r," approximately in metre-angles; consequently "r" equals the abducting power of the external recti. If no prism can be borne "r" = 0, and if "R" is at finite distance, its position can be ascertained by the dynamometer.

Schiötz, of Christiania, considers the "fusion far point to be equal to a prism of 8° base in, which is the strongest one (taking the average) that the external recti can overcome in order to maintain simultaneous binocular vision. This is a little more than 1 m.a. of divergence capacity." He further says: "Our far point for simultaneous vision with both eyes (fusion far point) must be that point at which our visual lines intersect *when we exert our externi to their utmost*"[1] (the italics are mine). But in normal distant vision our aim is parallelism, and we do not require to exert our externi to their utmost, and as we do not want to ascertain the actual abducting power of the externi, but their relative power, the latent position of the eyes at rest will give us our fusion far point. There is a great difference between the "region" of total convergence and the "range" of active convergence. If we take "r" as the maximum of divergence, or as Landolt calls it, the minimum of convergence, this "r" added to the total active convergence will give us the total convergence, but only part of it will be active, the remainder, the first part, will be only a relaxation of the divergence; whereas if we take "r" as representing the amount of deviation of the eyes at rest, if the latent position of the eyes at rest is one of divergence, the whole of the convergence will be active, although part of it (the first part) is negative. It is the range of active convergence, positive and negative (if the latter exists), that we wish to ascertain in treating convergence strain.

To find "p," the maximum of convergence, we direct the person to fix binocularly a small test object held, say, one-third metre from the eyes, equi-distant between them and on the horizontal plane of the eyes. This may be a fine hair or wire stretched vertically in a frame, or it may be a luminous slit, as in Landolt's dynamometer; when the object is approached to such a distance that the test line appears double we measure off the distance in centimetres, and dividing this into 100 gives us the number of metre-angles that "p" is equal to. Suppose "P" was 7 cms., then "p" $= \frac{100}{7} = 14$ m.a., and if R was at infinity

$$a = 14 - \infty = 14$$

if r $= -1$ m.a.

$$a = 14 - (-1) = 14 + 1 = 15 \text{ m.a.}$$

---

[1] *Knapp's Arch.*, vol. xix., p. 158.

CONVERGENCE.

In this test we must be careful to distinguish between mere haziness of the test object (which is the result of its being within the person's accommodation near point) and doubling of it, because the near point of convergence is often nearer than that of accommodation. We should therefore always first ascertain the accommodation near point in each eye.

It is generally considered that the normal amplitude of convergence is 10.5 m.a., although it may be 15 or even 17 m.a.

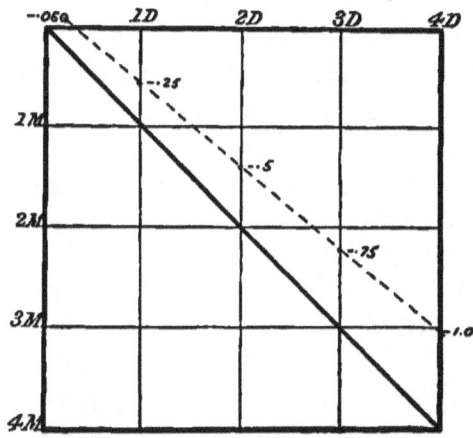

FIG 13 (after Berry).

Schiötz considers that the "fusion near point," as he calls it, is in normal binocular vision 6 cms. from the eyes.[1]

The Relative Range of Accommodation and Convergence.—Berry[2] points out that if the *latent* position of the eyes be tested, not only during the fixation of distant objects and of objects at a reading distance, but also for intermediate distances of fixation, it will be found that as a rule there is

---

[1] *Knapp's Arch. of Oph.*, vol. xix., p. 160.
[2] *Trans. Oph. Soc.*, vol. xi., p. 159.

quite a gradual lagging of the non-fixing eye behind the fixing one, a *gradual* increase of latent divergence. This divergence is greater in myopia and less in hypermetropia than in emmetropia. Fig. 13 represents the average curve of relative latent deviation in emmetropia.

According to this figure we see that with parallelism, or a condition almost approaching to parallelism for a distance, there is $\frac{1}{2}$ a metre angle of divergence on accommodating for $\frac{1}{2}$ metre, and a whole metre angle for $\frac{1}{4}$ metre accommodation. That is, that whereas, with both eyes fixing, on accommodating for $\frac{1}{4}$ metre, 4 D. of accommodation is used, and both eyes converge to a point using 4 m.a. of convergence, when the possibility of fusion is removed, both eyes only converge to a point $\frac{1}{3}$ metre off, using 3 m.a. of convergence.

This is no proof of the existence of "insufficiency" of convergence —all it shows is that the intimate relation between accommodation and convergence is not absolute.

All the more, then, should we expect to get latent divergence for near points when there is initial latent divergence for distance. When there is initial latent divergence for distance, the "lagging" of the convergence behind the accommodation for near points is more marked than when the position of the eyes is parallelism, and this produces a "convergence insufficiency." We can ascertain the presence of latent deviation in near vision by the Maddox test. A scale is held $\frac{1}{4}$ metre from the eyes and a prism of 12° base up is held before the right eye. The scale consists of a horizontal line, in the centre of which is an arrow pointing upwards. The line is divided in degrees which are marked by figures, black on the right of the arrow, red on the left. Every $3\frac{1}{2}°$ from the arrow is marked by a small cross representing 1 m.a. The prism causes two lines and two arrows to be seen; the person is instructed to fix the upper arrow—or better, the fine print just below it—and if there is no latent deviation the two arrows are in a vertical line; but if the lower arrow points to the left (red side) of the upper arrow, there is latent divergence, and if to the right (black side), latent convergence for $\frac{1}{4}$ metre, the amount of deviation being read off on the scale.

Maddox[1] maintains as a result of his experiments that in near binocular vision there is always relative divergence, that is, convergence always lags behind accommodation; and he says the convergence is composed of three factors:

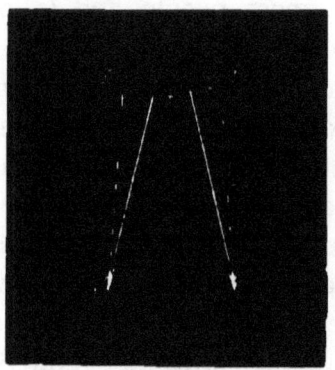

FIG. 14 (Maddox).

(1) "initial convergence" (this of course only exists when there is latent convergence) due to the relaxation of the external recti which are maintaining parallelism, p p (fig. 14), and the eyes assuming their position of rest i i; (2) accommodative convergence, *i.e.*, the amount of convergence which is called forth by the accommodative effort which brings the axes to a a; and lastly (3), the "fusion supplement" which is the result of the desire for single vision,

---

[1] *Oph. Rev.*, vol. v., p. 345.

and brings the axes to o. That Maddox is right with reference to what he calls the "fusion supplement," is demonstrated by holding a pen midway, before the eyes of a patient, at the distance of the convergence near point, and telling him to fix the tip of the pen; if now one eye is covered, this covered eye will markedly turn out, and on uncovering, the patient will for a moment have diplopia, the eye making an incursion to recover binocular vision. The amount of the excursion on covering, or incursion on uncovering, represents the fusion supplement which the demand for binocular vision calls forth. (This experiment can be made on most people, and is no proof of "insufficiency" of convergence.)

Although accommodation and convergence are intimately connected, this connection is not absolute. "It is easy to convince oneself that both eyes together, as well without, as with, slightly concave or convex glasses, can accurately see an object at a definite distance, and that, consequently, without change of convergence, the accommodation can be modified. With equal ease, we observe that in holding a weak prism before the eye, whether with the refracting angle turned inwards or outwards, an object can be accurately seen with both eyes at the same distance, and that, consequently, the convergence may be altered without modifying the accommodation" (Donders).[1]

Donders and Nagel[2] have shown that the amount of dissociation between the accommodative and convergence efforts is limited, and varies *with* and *in* the individual; that it could be increased by practice, and that it differed for varying degrees of accommodation and convergence. Fig.

---

[1] *Op. cit.*, p. 110.
[2] *Graefe-Sæmisch: Handbuch der Augenheilkunde*, bd. vi., p. 491.

15 shows the relative amount of accommodation that can be used with different degrees of convergence in an emmetrope aged 15.

The horizontal lines record the degrees of convergence, the figures representing metre angles, and the vertical lines record the degrees of accommodation, the figures representing dioptres. The diagonal D D represents the convergence,

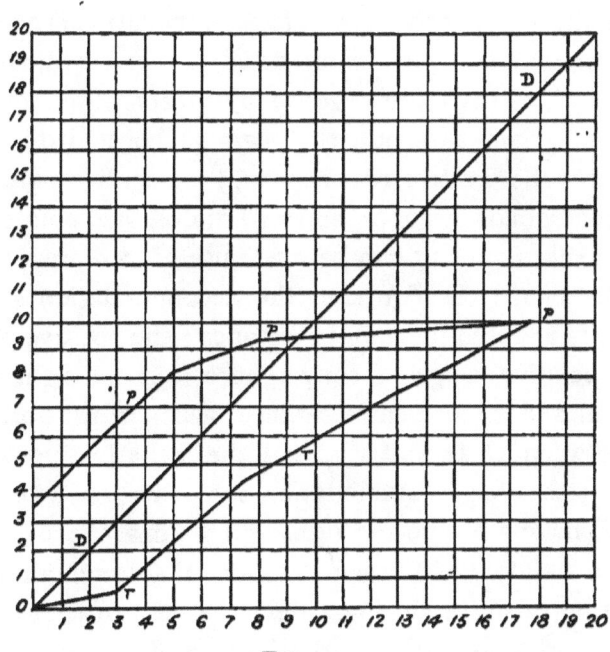

FIG. 15.

starting from zero, *i.e.*, infinity, and stopping at 5 cms. (20 metre angles). The division of the vertical lines between the upper curved line, p p, and the diagonal represent the amount of maximum or positive part of accommodation ascertained by the strongest concave glass that can "be borne without prejudice to binocular and distinct vision" for any given point of convergence, and the divisions of the vertical lines between the diagonal and the lower curved line r r represent the amount of minimum or negative part of accommodation ascertained by the strongest convex glass. Thus take convergence for 6 m.a., above we have 2.5 dioptres of positive accommodation, and below 3 D. of negative accommodation; that is, the relative amplitude of accommodation for 6 m.a. of convergence is 5.5 D. in this individual. It will be seen that when the convergence has reached 10 m.a. the whole of the range of accommodation is negative.

Accommodation remaining fixed, we can estimate the amount of relative convergence by means of prisms; the strongest prism base out, that can be borne with fusion represents the positive, and base in, the negative part of the amplitude of convergence, and as Landolt has pointed out, we find that figure 15 can be made use of to represent this. The diagonal D D represents the accommodation starting with eyes adapted for infinite distance; the positive portion of the relative range of convergence is to the right of the diagonal, and is represented by the division of the horizontal line between D D and r r, and the negative portion to the left; thus for accommodation at 25 cms., *i.e.*, 4 D., we see that we have 3 m.a. to the right and 3.5 m.a. to the left, that is, while maintaining the same amount of accommodation, an adducting prism producing a deviation of 3 m.a., and an abducting prism requiring a diminution of 3.5 m.a., can be overcome by the eyes. Thus for 4 D. of accommodative power in this individual an amplitude of convergence of 6.5 m.a. exists.

It is fortunate for the ametrope that this dissociation between accommodation and convergence is possible.

A hyperope of 3 D. who fixes an object binocularly 33 cms. off must use an additional 3 D. of accommodation, that is, he must use 6 D. altogether, but he will only require to converge to 3 m.a. . If the association between accommodation and convergence were absolute, he would either have to converge to 6 m.a., and consequently squint, and thus lose binocular vision, or he can keep binocular vision on the condition that he does not accommodate for this near point; in other words, he has the choice between distinct vision and binocular vision—he cannot have both. A large number of hyperopes dissociate these two efforts, and can by practice and "nerve education" accommodate in excess of their convergence (see page 70).

The same necessity for dissociation between convergence and accommodation occurs in myopia. A myope of 3 D. can see an object 33 cms. off without any accommodation, but he must converge to the extent of 3 m.a. Thus he uses his *convergence* in excess of his accommodation.

An individual whose ametropia is undoubtedly inherited, is less likely to be unfavourably situated in the association of his accommodative and convergent efforts, than one in whom the error of refraction is more distinctly accidental, and when changes take place in the refraction, the more rapid these changes, the less easy will be the corresponding adaptation (Berry).

The difference in the power to dissociate these two efforts, is the explanation of the well-known fact, that of two individuals having the same refractive defect, one will squint and the other not.

IV. **MUSCULAR INSUFFICIENCY.**—We have seen that in ideal binocular vision the visual axes are parallel when the eyes are at rest, E R (fig. 16, A), and that when the eyes accommodate for a point P, both eyes converge to that point, and that in normal vision, if we destroy the possibility of fusion, that convergence lags behind accommodation, and instead of converging for P, the visual axes are in the direction E A (fig. 16, B), and that the difference between A and P is the "fusion supplement;" and we have

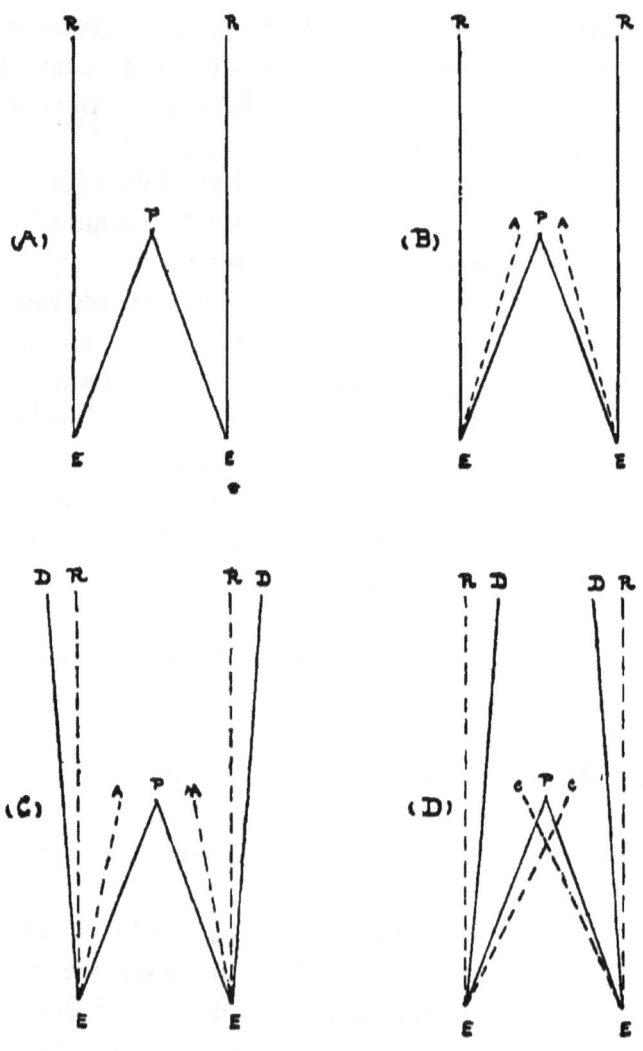

FIG. 16.

also seen that if the position of rest is one of divergence (fig. 16, C), A is further removed from P, and the "fusion supplement" is larger. Now this position of divergence at rest is caused by "muscular insufficiency," in this case, of the internal recti muscles. This means that the internal recti are insufficient to produce parallelism without active muscular contraction, which the demand for binocular vision necessitates during all the waking hours; hence the muscles are never at rest, and when the necessity for convergence arises, the interni start with a deficit of power. The constant using up of part of the convergence power fatigues the internal recti muscles, and the positive part of the amplitude of convergence will be found very much diminished. Landolt says, "In all cases where the positive convergence does not reach nine metre-angles, asthenopic troubles may become developed when the eyes are used for near vision. This is, of course, the more apt to happen, the more the maximum of this function falls below the given measure."[1]

The amplitude of convergence may be quite up to the average, but if the positive part of it is too small, this indicates the presence of insufficiency of the internal recti, and the liability to asthenopia. Take a patient who has 3 m.a. of latent divergence, and whose convergence near point is 14 cms; we have

$$ca = 7-(-3)$$
$$= 7+3$$
$$= 10 \text{ m.a.}$$

10 m.a. of amplitude of convergence would be quite sufficient if it were all positive, but only 7 are positive and only from $\frac{1}{3}$ to $\frac{1}{4}$ of this power should be used for any length of time, which means that only about 2 m.a. should be used, which would be useless for near work. Remove the in-

---

[1] *Op. cit.*, p. 506.

sufficiency, that is, remove his latent divergence, and he will not only have then 10 m.a. of positive convergence power, but even more, for the constant fatigue of the internal recti, produced by the work of overcoming the latent divergence, will be removed.

The term "insufficiency" has been used in such vague ways, that it is most important to define accurately what we mean by it. There are two kinds of "insufficiency:"—

1. Due to *relative* weakness of a muscle.

Insufficiency of a muscle due to *relative* weakness means that "a particular muscle is *relatively* weaker than its opponent, so that in 'static' and 'dynamic' vision extra impulses have to pass to that muscle in order to produce perfect fusion." An "insufficient" muscle is not necessarily weak. It is insufficient because its opponent, through spasm or preponderance (uebergewicht, as Graefe calls it) is "*too sufficient;*" hence in the case of "insufficiency" of the interni, although the muscles may be insufficient for convergence, they may be perfectly able to take their part in the associated movements of the eyes to either side.

2. Due to *absolute* weakness of a muscle, either of local or central origin.

Insufficiency may mean, especially in reference to convergence — commonly called convergence insufficiency — inability of the muscle to act normally irrespective of its opponent; thus Landolt[1] mentions a case of a neurasthenic where there was no latent divergence, *i.e.*, no negative portion of convergence, and yet the total amplitude of convergence only amounted to 3 m.a. (fig. 21 c). Here, through some central disturbance of either innervation or the power of fusion, the internal recti were insufficient.

---

[1] "Accommodation and Refraction," p. 504.

The patient appeared to have no power to supply a "fusion supplement."

Insufficiency may be present in any of the muscles; if the visual axes at rest are convergent, the external recti muscles are "insufficient" to produce parallelism (fig. 16, D). In this case, binocular distant vision, which should be perfect rest to the eyes, necessitates the constant contraction of the external recti, and they are liable to become fatigued and cause eyestrain; and also, during convergence we may find latent convergence, the eyes converging to a point nearer than P (fig. 16 D), and the necessity for fusion demands contraction of the external recti to overcome this over-action of the interni, hence fatigue. And so with the other muscles—if one muscle by spasm or preponderance over its opponent, prevents the eyes from assuming the normal position when at rest, there is liability to fatigue the asthenopia; whether it manifests itself or not (there are a large number of cases of insufficiency which never produce any symptoms) depends entirely on the amount of insufficiency, and the nervous condition of the individual.

When we consider that on the *relative* strength of the muscles of the eyeball depends the position of the eye, and that the smallest amount of preponderating strength, or the slightest amount of weakness of one muscle, will cause a displacement, or a tendency to displacement (*i.e.*, a latent deviation) of the eyes, we can only wonder that the condition of parallelism of the visual axes in distant vision is so constantly found. The secret is, that the desire for binocular vision, obtained by the fusion of the two images, acts as an unconscious stimulus to the weaker muscle, and masks the relative weakness. If binocular vision is impossible through the sight of one eye being very much inferior, then the stimulus is absent and the eyes assume a divergent or convergent position of rest, which becomes manifest and is then a squint. We must be careful not to use the term insufficiency in connection with squint; it is quite unnecessary, and causes a great deal of confusion to apply the term to, for instance, an atrophied internal rectus in an old divergent strabismus. An insufficiency, if unrelieved, may pass into a squint, just as congestion may pass into inflammation, but they are two distinct things.

In estimating insufficiency of a muscle we must beware of attaching too much importance to *one* examination; a muscle may be insufficient at one time and not at another.

The following experiment which I performed on myself illustrates this:—

Experiment.—Initial latent lateral deviation = o, that is, with the Maddox distance test the vertical streak of light passed through the candle. I then held before one eye a prism 12° base out for several minutes. On using the Maddox test I found latent convergence $\frac{1}{4}$ m.a. I had produced spasm of the internal recti, and consequent insufficiency of the externi. The normal power of my external recti is equal to a prism 8° base in, before one eye. I found that even with 6° I was unable to procure fusion. I obtained fusion with 3°, after a short time with 4°, and finally with 5°. I found then with the Maddox test that the spasm had disappeared and with it the insufficiency, and my latent lateral deviation was again o, and I was able to fuse with prism 8°. I held this prism 8° base in, for several minutes before the eye until the muscle gave way from fatigue, and then I found latent convergence for distance = 1 m.a., and at $\frac{1}{4}$ metre, $\frac{1}{2}$ m.a. (at this distance my normal condition is $\frac{1}{4}$ m.a. divergence). Thus in a short time I had produced insufficiency of the external rectus, first by spasm of the opponent and later on by fatigue of the muscle itself. These experiments were tried several times with practically the same result. Insufficiency of the superior and inferior recti was also produced in the same way.

Stevens has suggested the employment of the following terms in designating the condition of the extrinsic muscles of the eye:—

Orthophoria = visual axes parallel and lying in the horizontal plane.

Heterophoria = visual axes not parallel or not in the horizontal plane; divided into:

i. Exophoria. The eyes tend to turn out; insufficiency of the interni.

ii. Esophoria. The eyes tend to turn in; insufficiency of externi.

iii. Hyperphoria. One eye tends to be on a higher level than the other, due to insufficiency of the superior or inferior rectus.

iv. Insufficiency of the oblique muscles:

(*a*) Hyperesophoria, a tendency up and in.

(*b*) Hyperexophoria, a tendency up and out.[1]

(i.) *Exophoria.* Insufficiency of the internal recti—convergence strain.

V. Graefe says: "Another source of asthenopia is quite unconnected with accommodative work, and lies in the relative strength (Spannungsverhaeltnissen) of the internal recti." He only recognises insufficiency of these muscles in the dynamic condition, which Stevens calls exophoria in accommodation. This condition may exist, as we have seen on page 119, with latent divergence for distance, and this is the rule; but the visual axes may be parallel, or latent convergence may be present. Stevens says, that when this latter condition is present, that is, when esophoria is present for distance and exophoria in accommodation, hyperphoria is to be suspected as a complication, and he found it present in a very considerable proportion of cases.[2]

V. Graefe says: "One can define insufficiency"—*i.e.*, "convergence insufficiency"—"as a dynamic external

---

[1] "Functional Nervous Diseases," 1887, p. 192.
[2] *Knapp's Arch. of Oph.*, vol. xviii., p. 376.

squint (Auswaertsschielen) (varying with the distance from the object looked at) which is overcome for the time being by the strong desire for single vision."[1]

Strain of the internal recti is essentially dependent upon binocular vision, and persons who have not the advantage of binocular vision, by a compensation of nature, cannot suffer from this trouble.

Tests for Insufficiency of the Interni.—We have seen that the Maddox test is the best and simplest. If we find latent divergence for distance, or latent divergence of more than a metre-angle at $\frac{1}{4}$ metre, or both, we can positively assert that the interni are insufficient, and we can confirm this by ascertaining the amplitude of convergence, the ordinary working distance of the patient, and the reserve power of convergence.

Except in neurasthenic insufficiency, the estimation of the adducting power of the interni by prisms is not of much use. We may get an adducting power of 30° or 40°, and yet if the externi are "preponderating" we shall have insufficiency present.

If we direct a person suffering from convergence insufficiency to look at the tip of a pen held, say, 20 cms. from the eyes in the middle line, and gradually approach the pen to the eyes, a point will be reached when one of the eyes ceases to converge; it may make a few oscillations, due to the internal rectus trying to recover itself, and then it will turn slowly or suddenly out, and the point where this convergence ceases will be found to be further from the eyes than in a normal case, and it may be different at different times (see *Graefe's Arch.*, bd. 8., ii., p. 325).

Insufficiency of the interni is generally associated with myopia.

---

[1] *Graefe's Arch. f. Oph.*, band 8, ii., p. 345.

In spite of the statistics given by some American ophthalmologists, there is no doubt that convergence insufficiency is the commonest form of heterophoria. Burnett says that out of 50 recorded cases of heterophoria taken in succession from his case-book, 28 were exophoria, 18 esophoria, 3 hyperphoria and 1 combined eso- and hyperphoria.[1]

(ii.) *Esophoria. Insufficiency of the External Recti.*—
V. Graefe, Landolt, and most English writers entirely ignore this condition. On the other hand, several American writers place it at the head of the insufficiencies causing asthenopia. Noyes says that, out of 100 cases of muscular asthenopia, 92 were cases of insufficiency of externi![2] Roosa says that out of 103 patients examined who *had no trouble with their eyes*, no symptom of asthenopia or any other nervous phenomenon, 16 had insufficiency of the externi at rest.[3]

If latent convergence is demonstrated for distance, we say that we have "insufficiency" of the external recti, that is, in the position of rest the externi are relatively weak. If there is no manifest convergence the visual axes assume a parallel condition, when binocular vision is again possible. To maintain this, active contraction of the external recti must take place always, when distant vision is used, in order to prevent diplopia. Latent convergence is very common, but, in the majority of cases, gives rise to no symptoms. The explanation is, that the latent deviation is slight, and in our civilized state active use of the eyes is mostly associated with a necessary convergent condition.

---

[1] *Trans. American Oph. Soc.*, Annual Meeting, 1891, p. 221.
[2] *American Journal of Oph.*, vol. vii., p. 257.
[3] *New York Med. Journal*, 1890, vol. li.

When the latent convergence is excessive we may get symptoms of muscular asthenopia.

Test for Insufficiency of the Externi.—If the Maddox test reveals latent convergence for distance, or for $\frac{1}{4}$ metre, it is present.

The abducting power of normal externi is equal to a prism of 7° or 8°.

Insufficiency of the externi is generally associated with hyperopia.

(iii.) *Hyperphoria. Insufficiency of the superior or inferior rectus.*—To judge from the writings of American ophthalmologists, this is very much more common over the water than it is here.

I have proved hyperphoria of a very small amount, to be present in many cases that exhibited no symptoms of asthenopia. In the following case asthenopia *was* present, but it might have been due entirely to the refractive error.

Muscular Asthenopia.—Neurasthenia.—Insufficiency of the External Recti.—Hyperphoria.

O. C., aged 10, an anæmic nervous boy, complains of strain of the eyes after school work.

$$V < \begin{array}{l} R = \frac{6}{6} + 1 D = Hm. \\ L = \frac{6}{6} + 3 D = \frac{6}{24}. \end{array}$$

The shadow test under atropine shows

$$R = + 2.5 D.$$
$$L = + + 3 D.$$
$$+ 3.5 D.$$

Ordered R + 1.5 D sph.
L + 3 D sph.
+ .5 D cyl. axis horizontal.

He has latent convergence for distance of 2 m.a.; at times this manifests itself as a converging squint. He has hyperphoria of $\frac{3}{4}$ m.a., due to insufficiency of the left inferior rectus. He is sent into the country in order to improve his health and insure rest to the eyes, and the glasses are ordered for constant use.

Seen two months later, his external rectus insufficiency was reduced by one-half, being only 1 m.a., and his hyperphoria had almost disappeared, and he complained no more of eyestrain.

Brailey records two cases. One patient was 30, and for many years had suffered from eyestrain. His refractive correction was − 1 D. cyl. and − 1 D. sph. for distance, and the cylinder alone for reading. On examination with prisms it was found that when, by their use, the images were separated laterally, that of the right was always lower than the left by two inches.[1] The other was a girl, aged 16, who had hyperopic astigmatism, and whose right image was six inches lower than the left.[2]

Stevens[3] gives an analysis of 200 cases of this muscular anomaly, in 100 of which no disease or injury of the eyes was found, and in which the refractive errors were not sufficient to account for the trouble. Of the 200, 45 were emmetropes, and 81 had normal acute vision. He mentions as a peculiar feature of this form of muscular asthenopia, the inability to see small objects clearly, although for larger objects the vision is good. The fault, he considers, is due to the inability to fuse the two images, while the separation is not sufficiently great to enable the patient easily to suppress one of them.

Amidon reports two cases of insufficiency of the superior rectus of one eye. The symptoms were constant headache, nausea, vomiting and vertigo ; both were in gentlemen who suffered from bad health, one was suffering from hyperopia and presbyopia, and the other from hyperopic astigmatism.[4]

(iv.) *Insufficiency of the Oblique Muscles.*—Savage[5] appears

---

[1] *Trans. Oph. Soc.*, vol. i., p. 188.
[2] *Trans. Oph. Soc.*, vol. iii., p. 288.
[3] *Knapp's Arch. of Oph.*, vol. xvi., p. 161.
[4] *New York Medical Record*, April, 1887, p. 462.
[5] *Knapp's Arch. of Oph.*, vol. xx., p. 105.

to have seen cases of "insufficiency" of the oblique muscles. This is the result of the superior oblique of either eye being too strong for its inferior, or *vice versâ*. The parallelism of the vertical meridians of the corneæ is maintained by the equilibrium of these muscles; hence, if one muscle is weaker, excessive work must be put upon it in order to preserve the parallelism, and Savage says that a train of nervous symptoms are thus brought on, for which at present there seems no hope of cure.

The presence of these insufficiencies is revealed by the Maddox glass rod test (see *Oph. Rev.*, vol. ix., p. 129, "A New Test for Heterophoria").

V. CAUSES OF MUSCULAR ASTHENOPIA.

Muscular asthenopia is much less common than ciliary asthenopia. I have notes of 94 cases of the former as against 323 of the latter. V. Graefe said that out of 100 eye-patients presenting themselves to him, about 10 suffered from asthenopia, and of these 10, one was a case of muscular asthenopia.[1]

Heterophoria, the result of muscular insufficiency, in most cases lies at the bottom of the causes of muscular asthenopia.

Table of Causes.

IN EMMETROPIA, due to :—
    i. Abuse in the healthy (excessive or prolonged convergence).
    ii. Nervo-muscular debility :
        (*a*) Neurasthenia.
        (*b*) General debility.
    iii. Congenital defect.

IN AMETROPIA, in :—
    i. Hyperopia (high).
    ii. Myopia.
    iii. Astigmatism.
    iv. Anisometropia.

---

[1] *Graefe, Arch.*, bd. 8, ii., p. 322.

VI. In **EMMETROPIA**. *In the Healthy.*—As ciliary strain generally accompanies convergent strain, the remarks on page 35 apply equally here. It is difficult to distinguish sometimes between the two forms (see Graefe's differential symptoms, page 31). Ciliary strain is more common than the latter, as we should expect, for the internal recti can stand more strain without showing fatigue, than the delicate ciliary muscles. In practice, our examples of muscular asthenopia under this heading are mostly jewellers and engravers, who do not use a "watchmaker's glass" and sit at very fine work for many hours a day.

Neurasthenic Muscular Asthenopia.—This is the central motor-asthenopia of Landolt. Neurasthenics exhibit inability to maintain prolonged convergence, through the increased tendency to fatigue of the internal recti, which share in the loss of nerve power of the rest of the system. The total amplitude of convergence is often very small.

Neuropathic Muscular Asthenopia occurs in those recovering from severe illness, or suffering from anæmia, or any other debilitating constitutional disease (see remarks on page 38).

Congenital Defect.—V. Graefe believed that congenital preponderance (uebergewicht) of the externi was at the bottom of most cases of insufficiency of the interni. He says:[1] " Es scheint, dass meist ein angeborenes uebergewicht der externi zu Grunde liegt, welches sich auch *heriditär* fortpflanzt."

The externus may be inserted too far forward, or the internus too far back. This may occur in any condition of the eye, but is generally associated with ametropia. (See paper by Lawford on "Congenital Hereditary Defect of Ocular Movements."[2])

---

[1] *Graefe, Arch.,* bd. 8, ii., p. 339.
[2] *Trans. Oph. Soc.,* vol. viii., p. 262.

Treatment. — The treatment of those whose sight is normal, and whose muscular asthenopia is due to simple fatigue, consists simply in directing them to put their work further back, and the remarks on page 45 with reference to ciliary asthenopia from the same cause, are equally applicable here.

One thing is very important — when we give these patients a low convex glass, our object is to make larger images, and enable the work to be put further back, and if the patients do not distinctly understand this, they will be tempted to approach their work nearer to the eyes, which of course will aggravate, instead of remedy the strain.

Orthoptic training, or gymnastic exercises, devised by Dr. Dyer in connection with the ciliary muscles (see page 49), can be with very great benefit extended to the extrinsic muscles. For strengthening the internal recti we employ properly regulated convergence for a short time at different periods of the day, which time is to be gradually increased as the muscles increase in strength, measured of course by the tests previously cited. For strengthening the external recti we must employ prisms with their base in. The best plan is to provide the patient with a square prism, say 2°, and tell him to practise fusion several times a day, and when this is accomplished with ease, we can increase the strength of the prism in the same way until the "insufficiency" disappears.

When the muscular asthenopia is the result of defective or enfeebled muscles, we must first of all improve the general health by enjoining out-door exercise and attention to the bowels, and by the administration of tonics, and then, remembering that absolute rest will only tend to increase the weakness, we must commence regular exercise of convergence (if we are dealing with "convergence insufficiency") for short periods, gradually increased, and forbid the patient to use the eyes for near work except at these times. To carry out this treatment in young subjects the use of a mydriatic is most helpful. Forced or prolonged efforts of convergence would only help to increase the fatigue of the internal recti, and therefore we must commence with very short efforts, and increase those efforts very slowly.

Doyne has described a stereoscope, which is very useful for the orthoptic training of the eyes.[1]

As a last resource weak prisms, with their base in, may be tried for convergence insufficiency; with their help the convergence effort is diminished, but all hope of the muscles regaining their normal condition must be given up, unless the prisms are only used temporarily while the general condition is being improved.[2] Prisms employed in this way never *cure* " insufficiency," they *relieve* it.

Noyes reports[3] one hundred cases of muscular asthenopia in which prisms were employed, and out of these complete relief occurred in 74 cases, moderate relief in 5, no relief in 13, temporary relief in 6. In the larger number of cases prisms were worn constantly. The refraction of the hundred cases was as follows:—Emmetropia in 47; hyperopia in 25; astigmatism in 27; anisometropia in 1. The condition of the muscles was as follows:—Insufficiency of the externi in 92; of the interni in 7; and general insufficiency in 1.

Brailey has reported two cases where the use of prisms gave great relief. The first was a delicate child aged 7, in whom asthenopic symptoms were immediately and per-

---

[1] *Oph. Rev.*, vol. vii., p. 65.
[2] See Sect. X. (on prisms).
[3] *American Journal of Ophthalmology*, vol. vii., p. 257.

fectly relieved by the use of a prism, 4° base in, divided between the two eyes. Both internal and external recti were absolutely weak, the latter apparently even more so than the former. There was no hyperopia.[1] Amidon's cases of insufficiency of the superior rectus were relieved by prisms[2] (see further, Sect. X.)

Treatment by Traction.

Placing the eye under the influence of cocaine, seizing the conjunctiva and sclerotic over the stronger muscle with a pair of fixation forceps, and pulling over the eye as far as possible towards the weaker antagonist, has been recommended ; by this means the preponderating muscle is stretched and weakened.

VII. MUSCULAR ASTHENOPIA IN AMETROPIA:
Hyperopia.

(*a*) Insufficiency of the internal recti, generally the result of fatigue from excessive convergence, occurs (i.) in young hyperopes suffering from spasm of the ciliary muscle, and thus made artificially myopic. The eyes are focussed for very near work, and consequently undue convergence has to be exercised in order to see binocularly. (ii.) In high hyperopia; to supply the deficiency of distinctness, the patient approaches his eyes very near his work in order to get larger retinal images. Here again the patient strains his convergence.

(*b*) Insufficiency of the external recti. We have seen that in hyperopia, accommodation is required in excess of convergence, and unless the two can be dissociated the hyperope must converge to a nearer point than he requires to. This over-contraction of the interni causes latent convergence for distance, and also the near point (fig. 16 D.), the external recti become insufficient, and extra impulses must pass down to these muscles in order to obtain fusion

---

[1] *Trans. Oph. Soc.*, vol. iii., p. 287.
[2] *New York Med. Rec.*, Ap., 1887.

vision. This may lead to fatigue, and all the symptoms of asthenopia, which, however, rapidly disappear if nature is allowed to effect the cure, which, as we have seen, means the development of a squint and loss of binocular vision; and for this reason asthenopia, as a result of insufficiency of the externi in hyperopia, is not at all common, although some American ophthalmologists claim that it is.

Treatment.

Convergence Insufficiency.—The regular instillation of atropine, and proper correction of the error of refraction, with special injunction to cease for some time from all close work, will remove the strain. The high hyperope will find that suitable glasses will enable him to put back his work considerably, and thus remove the strain on his convergence.

Insufficiency of the Externi.—By putting the hyperope into glasses, we re-establish the harmony between convergence and accommodation, remove the spasm of the internal recti, and consequently also the insufficiency of the externi, restoring the balance of all the muscles. One of the pleasantest things to do in ophthalmic work is to cure a squint, or a tendency to squint, by simply giving the patient glasses. If parents would only realize that, in a large number of cases, this can be done by bringing the child early enough, *i.e.*, before the latent squint has become manifest, or it may be during the early period of the manifest squint, there would be fewer squints in the world.

VIII. MYOPIA ($\mu\acute{u}\epsilon\iota\nu$, to close, $\H{\omega}\psi$, the eye, from the habit of myopes of partially shutting the eyes in order to cut off the rays of diffusion), or short-sight, is a condition of the eye in which the antero-posterior diameter is too long, so that parallel rays come to a focus in front of the retina (fig. 6 M.), and only divergent rays from near objects (fig. 17) or parallel rays made divergent by a concave glass (fig. 18) can be made to focus on the retina. Roughly speaking, every dioptre of myopia means a lengthening of the antero-posterior axis of the eye by about $\frac{1}{3}$ of a millimetre. The punctum remotum of a

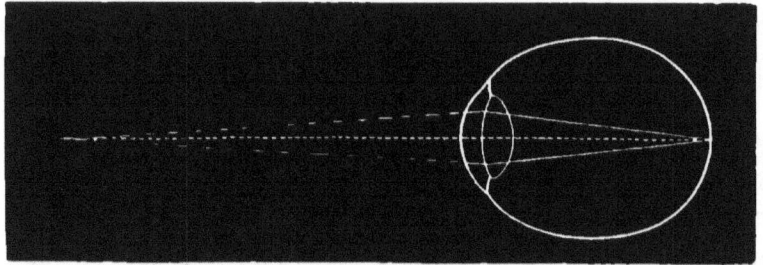

FIG. 17.

myope is always at a finite distance, the distance being measured by the amount of myopia. Thus a myope of 1 D. has his far point one metre from the eye, a myope of 2 D. has his far point half a metre, or 50 cms., and a myope of 5 D.,

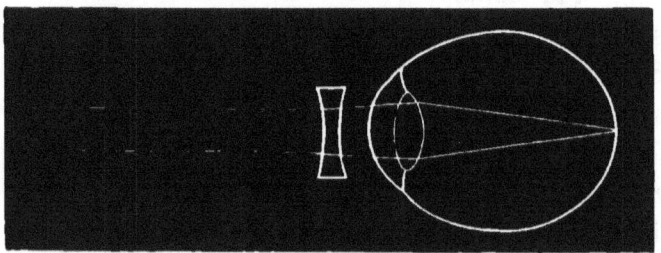

FIG. 18.

20 cms. from the eye. A myope of 5 D. can see a point 20 cms. from the eye without using his accommodation, but he must converge to 5 m.a. in order to see binocularly. As a compensation for the visual defect, most myopes have the power of using their convergence in excess of their ac-

commodation, just as a hyperope has often the power of using his accommodation in excess of his convergence; but as we have seen (p. 70), they both have to pay a penalty for this, the liability to strain always being greater when either effort is used in excess of the other. The "fusion supplement" must be greater than in emmetropia, and *the greater the "fusion supplement" the greater the fatigue to the internal recti;* the fatigue leads to "insufficiency" of the muscles, and matters are made worse. But it is not only the *excess* of convergence, but the *excessive* convergence that tends to produce strain and fatigue of the internal recti. The uncorrected myope sees nothing distinctly beyond his far point, and if he wishes to see clearly he must bring everything within that point; for instance, an emmetrope wishes to know the time by the clock, he can see the hands across a room, but the myope must go up to the clock and bring it within his far point; and moreover the incentive to use this remedy is great because the remedy is perfect. A high hyperope has the same difficulty with distant objects, but he has not the same remedy. Naturally, the greater the myopia, the nearer is the far point, and the greater is the convergence strain.

A myope requires more convergence of the visual lines because vision takes place closer to the eyes, and as Donders has shown, precisely in myopia is this, for two reasons, more difficult, first on account of impeded movements due to the altered shape of the eyeball, which becomes ellipsoidal in form, and which, in turning round the short axis in a cavity of similar shape, gives rise to great resistance; and secondly, on account of the altered direction of the visual lines, the angle a (angle formed by the visual and optic axes) being smaller than in emmetropia or hyperopia. If a myope cannot dissociate his accommodation and convergence, he has the same difficulties as a hyperope; he can either see distinctly but sacrifice binocular vision to remove the diplopia, or he can use his accommodation when he does not require it, and see indistinctly. We see, then, that fatigue and insufficiency of the internal recti is especially associated with myopia. Hence this form of ametropia is a very fruitful source of asthenopia, although in my experience it ranks lowest of all the errors of refraction in causing eyestrain. I found asthenopia present in 23 per cent. of myopia (fig. 2, p. 29). The American table (fig. 1) shows strain to have been present in 60 per cent. of myopia, whereas hyperopic asthenopia was only 35 per cent.

Treatment.—We thoroughly test our patient under atropine by the shadow test, &c. (see page 44). When the patient is out of atropine we find that we can generally increase the atropine correction by − 1 D. for the same reason that we decreased it by the same amount in hyperopia (many surgeons in both cases always keep to the atropine correction). In all cases of slight myopia, the glasses should be given to wear always. We thus make the patient practically emmetropic. He uses his accommodation instead of letting it remain idle, and he has no need to bring his work too close, and experience has proved that this has a decidedly deterrent effect in the progressive character of the myopia. Priestley Smith says: " My present custom is to encourage rather than to discourage, with proper limits, the use of the accommodation, in other words, to advise those who can, to use the *same glasses* for reading and for distance, and where this is impossible, by reason of weak accommodation, still to give reading glasses as strong as can be worn with comfort."[1]

---

[1] B.M.A. Meeting, Birmingham, 1890.

By fully correcting the myopia we restore the harmony between the accommodation and convergence efforts, but for this very reason, although the treatment is almost always practicable in young people, older patients refuse it. The habit of converging in excess of their accommodation has become so fixed that it cannot, even by practice, in many be disturbed, and if we insist on this correction for near work, we *create strain* instead of remove it. As a matter of fact, distance glasses for these, need be the sole treatment, if the myopia does not exceed, say, 5 D. We must remember that there are many persons with a myopia of 3 D. who never use glasses all their life; they put up with the indistinct distant images, and learn to recognise them, and their near work need not be near enough to cause any convergence strain.

It is most important, in giving concave glasses for near work, to insist on the work being held at a good distance, not nearer than 33 cms. from the eyes, otherwise we not only fail to remove the convergence strain, but render the patient liable to accommodation strain, for the myope's ciliary muscle is weaker, and therefore more liable to fatigue, than that of an emmetrope or hyperope.

If the myope will not bear the full correction, we take off, for near work, the amount of dioptres that represents the amount of accommodation required; for instance, if a person has myopia of 9 D., and wishes to work at 25 cms., we take off 4 D. and give him — 5 D. for near work; if he wishes to work at 33 cms., we give him — 6 D. In very high myopia we often find that the patient will not bear the full correction even for distance.

Landolt, on the other hand, says : " A myope must be prohibited from wearing a concave glass for any distance at which he can see clearly without accommodation,"[1] and again he says, correcting glasses have a very serious disadvantage for the myope, because "they force him to make an effort of accommodation from which his ametropia grants him dispensation, and they deprive him of another advantage, *i.e.*, of the larger size of the retinal images obtained by the naked eye, and which the glasses make smaller."[2] But surely this excessive convergence is, as it were, Nature's compensation for the original defect, and we want to get rid of it, because not only is convergence strained but the stooping position of the head, which so often accompanies it, favours congestion and leads to increased intraocular pressure, which causes the myopia to increase; and thus by giving the myope such glasses that his reading or working distance is put back to 25 or 33 cms., we not only prevent eyestrain but also prevent the increase of his defect.

IX. ASTIGMATISM.—Myopic astigmatism takes the first place amongst refractive errors, as a cause of asthenopia, for we not only may have ciliary asthenopia, caused by the confusion of the images and the frequently varying accommodative effort (Brailey), and the unequal contraction of the ciliary muscle (Fick and Dobrowolsky), but we have also muscular asthenopia. We have seen that in astigmatism "according to the rule" the vertical meridian is the myopic one in simple and mixed astigmatism, and the most myopic one in compound astigmatism. Compound myopic astigmatism is by far the commonest of these. In 1891, at the Central London Ophthalmic Hospital, out of a total of 2,197 cases of errors of refraction, 205 suffered from this defect, whereas only 55 had mixed astigmatism, and 25

---

[1] *Op. cit.*, p. 490.   [2] *Op. cit.*, p. 486.

simple myopic astigmatism (see also figs. 1 and 2, page 28). By partially closing his eyes the sufferer from compound myopic astigmatism cuts off his vertical rays, and thus clears his images and makes himself a simple myope, and the greater the degree of his horizontal myopia, the nearer will be his far point, and the greater the convergence strain. Hence in astigmatism "contrary to the rule," when the horizontal myopia is higher, the liability to asthenopia is greater still.

Although convergence "insufficiency" is the commonest, any of the forms of "insufficiency" may be associated with astigmatism.

Amidon reported a case of hyperopic astigmatism in which "insufficiency" of the superior rectus of one eye was present.[1]

(For treatment see page 87).

Anisometropia.—It is only in the first variety of this defect, viz., where binocular vision exists, that muscular asthenopia may be present, and the cause really lies more in the refraction defect, such as myopia, than in the anisometropia.

Theobald relates some cases of muscular "insufficiencies" producing asthenopia, in astigmatic anisometropia, cured by the correction of the refraction errors.[2]

(For treatment see page 92).

X. TREATMENT BY PRISMS OR DECENTERING.

—When we cannot hope to restore the muscles of the eye to a practically normal condition, we may aid them and remove the asthenopia by giving prisms, or if glasses are worn, by combining with them prisms, or by decentering the glasses.

If the internal recti are insufficient, the prism should

---

[1] *New York Med. Rec.*, April, 1887, p. 462.
[2] *American Jour. of Ophth.*, vol. vii., p. 37.

be placed base inwards, or if decentering is preferred, concave glasses should be decentered outwards (fig. 19), and convex glasses decentered inwards, in both of which cases the part of the lens the patient looks through will be converted into a prism with its base inwards.

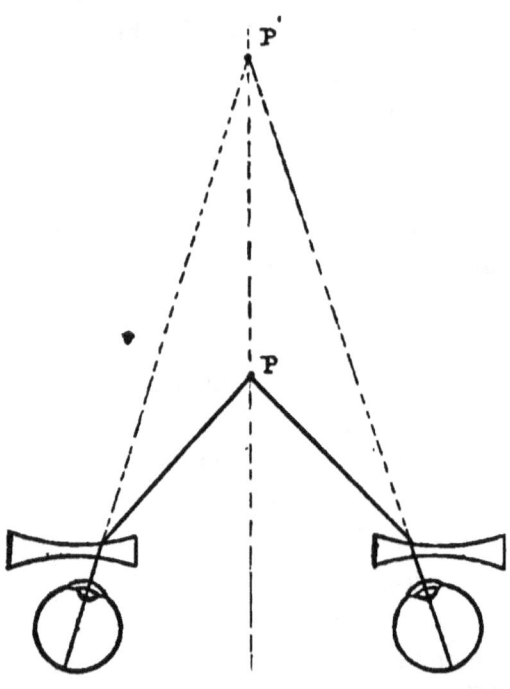

FIG. 19.

If the external recti are insufficient, the prism should be placed base outwards, concaves decentered inwards, and convexes outwards (fig. 20). If the superior or inferior rectus is "insufficient," the prism should be placed base up or down according to the effect required. Brailey, in both his cases of hyperphoria (see page 125), after correcting the error of refraction, gave a prism 3° which relieved the symptoms of muscular asthenopia. In the first case he gave the prism apex up before the right eye, and in the second, apex down before the left eye.

At the International Medical Congress, at Washington,

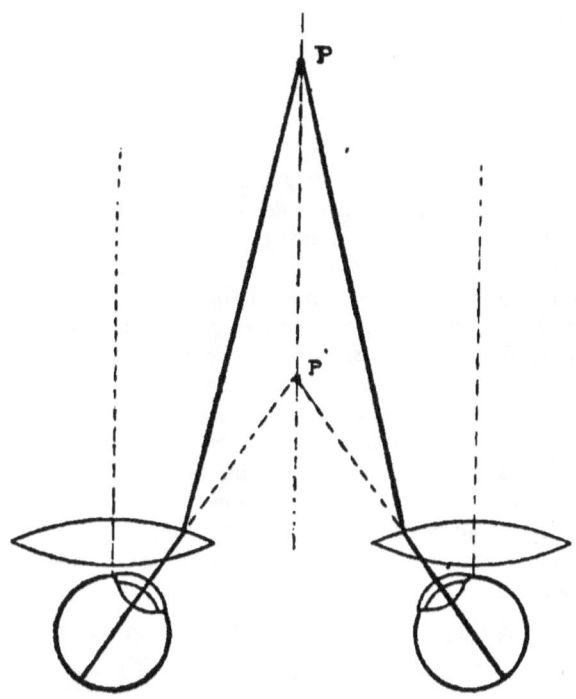

FIG. 20.

in 1887, Shakespeare reported that he corrected insufficiency of the superior or inferior rectus by means of prisms or decentered glasses (and not by tenotomy).[1]

Ward Holden gives a very easy method of finding the amount of decentering necessary to produce the effect of a given prism in a given lens.

---

[1] *Knapp's Arch.*, vol. xvii., p. 241.

Taking 8.7 mm. as the distance a lens of 1 D. must be moved to produce the effect of a prism 1° as the unit, he multiplies 8.7 mm. by the number of the prism, whose effect is required, and divides the product by the number of the lens, in dioptres. Thus the effect of a prism 3° in a lens 7 D. is obtained by decentering that lens to the extent of $\frac{8.7 \times 3}{7}$ mm. = 3.7 mm.[1]

The use of prisms is limited to about 4° in front of each eye, as any stronger prism than this would make the glasses too heavy.

Brudenell Carter, in his Hunterian Lectures, 1877, said that he had quite given up the use of prisms *when the range of accommodation was sufficient.* He assumes convergence to fifteen inches to be an invariable requirement, and modifies the concave lenses in such a way that the demand for accommodation shall be such as can most easily be combined with this invariable convergence. If a prism of 4° with its base inwards facilitates reading, we know the patient has been exerting too much convergence for the degree of his accommodation, and he increases the demand for accommodation by increasing the concave lens. If the prism with its base inwards increases the difficulty instead of diminishing it, it should be turned with its base outwards; if then it gives relief we know that the convergence was too little for the accommodation, and he diminishes the accommodation to the level of the convergence required, by weakening the concave lens.

XI. TREATMENT BY TENOTOMY.

—In America, graduated tenotomy of the preponderating muscle, (on one occasion performed thirteen times on the same muscle), is in favour among some oculists.

Fulton says, in writing on heterophoria, " The first and most important symptom is headache. I have now *operated* for heterophoria in some of its forms 260 times; of this number 190 suffered from headache. In a vast majority of cases the headache was cured, in nearly all relieved."

---

[1] *Knapp's Arch.*, vol. xx., p. 21.

He operates under cocaine in a dark room. A candle is placed twenty feet from the operating chair, and a focus of light is thrown by an assistant on the eye. He first makes a small hole in the tendon of the muscle, and judges of the amount of fibres to cut, by constant examination of the position of the eyes by placing before them a prism to produce diplopia. He says, "Fibre after fibre is thus cut until one candle comes over the other, or they are brought upon a level, as we require."

He advises that the operation should only be done for heterophoria if there are symptoms of asthenopia, which symptoms may be present "with half a degree of insufficiency of the internal recti in one person, while eight or ten degrees in another will not be noticed." He further advises that "other means should be resorted to before trying tenotomy, but unnecessary delays should be avoided."[1]

Burnett says: "If tenotomy will restore the lost equilibrium of the muscles it is certainly the most scientific, the readiest, and in every way, the most commendable method of dealing with the difficulty. My own experience with the operation is somewhat limited, but could have been greater had I been less conservative and cautious. The results, however, have been eminently satisfactory and such as to convince me that not only is it a legitimate operation, but one that, under certain circumstances, is imperatively demanded;" and he proceeds to give detailed notes of five cases where a "partial tenotomy" was successful.[2]

Stevens says,[3] "The treatment of hyperphoria is tenotomy." The surgeon must choose between operating on the superior rectus of one eye, or the inferior rectus of the

---

[1] *American Journal of Oph.*, vol. vii., p. 34.
[2] *Trans. Am. Oph. Soc.*, vol. vi., p. 221.
[3] *Knapp's Arch.*, vol. xvi., p. 171.

other, or in some cases, both. He says during the year 1886 he performed tenotomy for relief of hyperphoria 109 times in 88 cases. The result in nearly every instance was, when the patient was last examined, a relief, either partial or complete, to the hyperphoria.

David Webster, in a paper on "Tenotomies for Correction of Heterophoria,"[1] gives a detailed account of 40 cases in which he operated. The tenotomies were:—

Inferior rectus	3
Superior rectus	7
External rectus	19
Internal rectus	26

Most of the patients suffered from muscular asthenopia, with headache, &c., and these were either cured or greatly relieved (four were epileptics and they were *not* cured). He distinctly lays down the law that no operation should be performed unless troublesome symptoms are present, and then only when all other means for relief have failed.

Myles Standish[2] reports five cases of muscular asthenopia where partial tenotomy was done and gave great relief.

Epéron, in two cases of "insufficiency" of the superior obliques produced by local injury, effected complete cure of the diplopia by tenotomising the internal rectus of the same side and the inferior rectus of the opposite side.[3]

But "tenotomy mania" reaches its climax in the following paragraph, quoted from Stevens' article on the treatment of esophoria. He says:

"There may by the vertical prism be found no manifest esophoria, nor is hyperphoria shown by the horizontal prism,

---

[1] *Trans. American Oph. Soc.*, vol. v., p. 176.
[2] *Trans. American Oph. Soc.*, vol. v., p. 386
[3] *Oph. Rev.*, vol. viii., p. 207.

but the abduction power is less than the standard. If, after training the abducting muscles by requiring them to overcome gradually increasing prisms a few minutes at a time for several days, the abducting power remains too low, a weak prism may be worn for a few days with its base out. If even then there is no manifest esophoria, and the abducting power is the same or less, and if there is no exophoria in accommodation, *an operation is undoubtedly permissible*"[1] (the italics are mine); and he remarks that he would operate *even if the patient experienced no conscious discomfort* because the esophoria causes a waste of nervous power.

Comment is needless.

Again, Stevens confesses to having performed tenotomy for the relief of esophoria 2000 times!

Surely all the insufficiencies of the externi in the world must have found their way to him, and this is a condition very rarely met with here *as causing asthenopia*, and even then, glasses will cure it.

It will be interesting to learn, say, in ten years' time, the further history of those patients who have been so liberally dosed with tenotomy.

Writing in 1861, V. Graefe says: "Als eigentliches Heilmittel steht obenan die Tenotomie des externus."[2] and he gives several examples where good results followed division of the external rectus for convergence strain.

That in certain cases enormous benefit results from tenotomy, has been proved by Landolt, but he only advises surgical interference in certain picked cases.

He finds that in neurasthenics, neuropathics and those suffering from high myopia, where the convergence insuffi-

---

[1] *Knapp's Arch. of Oph.*, vol. xvii., p. 184.
[2] *Graefe's Arch.*, bd. viii., 2, p. 348.

ciency is due to very small amplitude of convergence, no good results from operation (fig. 21 c). But when the range of convergence is large, but too much of it is on the negative side, tenotomy of one or both externi or advancement of one or both interni cures the asthenopia, because it removes the negative convergence power to the positive side (see page 117). For instance, Landolt gives an example of a

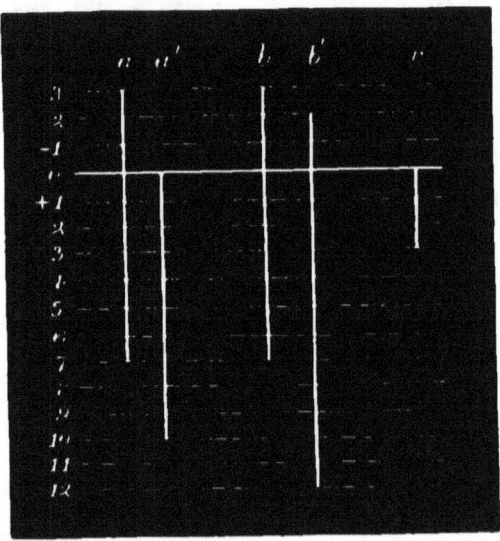

FIG. 21.

case (fig. 21 a) where before the operation there was 3 m.a. of divergence, and the convergence near point was 14 cms. off, with asthenopia. In this case $ca = \frac{100}{14} - (-3) = \frac{100}{14} + 3 = 10$ m.a., but only 7 of these 10 metre angles of convergence power were available; tenotomy of the external rectus removed the divergence, and the whole of the 10 m.a. became available and the asthenopia disappeared (fig. 21 a'). In the following case he obtained a still better result (fig. 21 b). A robust man, aged 30, had myopia of 6 D. in left and 7 D. in right eye, with astigmatism of 1.25 D. in each eye; after correction he still had insufficiency of convergence

$$c\ r = -3$$
$$c\ p = 7 \therefore ca = 10 \text{ m.a.}$$

After tenotomy of one externus

$$c\ r = -2$$
$$c\ p = 12 \therefore ca = 14 \text{ m.a.}$$

and we see he has 12 m.a. of convergence power available (fig. 21 b'). The asthenopia disappeared. Since the operation, the amplitude of accommodation had remained unchanged. Here 1 metre angle of divergence was sacrificed, and 5 m.a. of positive convergence gained.[1] Standing midway between these examples of peripheral motor asthenopia, and neurasthenic or central motor asthenopia, is a class of cases where the amplitude of convergence is decidedly below the average, and the internus is markedly weak; for these cases he advises advancement of one or both interni.

I have been on the look-out, for some time past, for a case of "peripheral motor asthenopia" that I could justifiably treat by tenotomy, but have failed to find one. The correction of the refraction error, constitutional treatment or orthoptic training, have in all cases cured the patient and disappointed (?) me of my operation.

XII. RECAPITULATION. — Muscular asthenopia is generally to be traced to some error of refraction which necessitates too close approximation of the eyes to the work, or in those who are normal-sighted to too prolonged application to near work; hence it is in a large number of cases due to strain on the convergence muscles of the eye *i.e.* the internal recti. Equilibrium of all the ocular muscles, producing complete parallelism of the

---

[1] *Op. cit.*, p. 506.

visual axes, is rare, but the amount of deviation in the majority of cases is so slight, that it produces no symptoms and can be ignored.

Muscular asthenopia occurs in two forms: one, "peripheral motor asthenopia," in which the balance of the ocular muscles is destroyed by the preponderance of one or more muscles, causing so-called "insufficiency" of the opponents, which muscles need not be abnormally weak; the other, "central motor asthenopia," due to actual weakness of the muscles which are insufficient. Insufficiency of the externi is generally associated with hyperopia, and of the interni with myopia.

The treatment consists essentially in removing the necessity for too great convergence. The correction of any error of refraction is of first importance. If this fails to remove the strain, orthoptic training of the insufficient muscle should be tried, with constitutional treatment. Tenotomy of the preponderating muscle is justifiable only when other means have failed, and then only in peripheral motor asthenopia, when the amplitude of convergence is not much diminished.

Correcting prisms can only relieve or remove the symptoms while they are in use, and for this reason should only be employed as a last resource. Decentering of the glasses may take the place of prisms.

Illustrative cases.—*Muscular Asthenopia from abuse.*

C. F., aged 36, a precious-stone setter, complains that his sight is failing, and that after work his eyes are painful, and his head aches. He does not use a watchmaker's glass, and sometimes works fourteen hours a day. His eyes show marked chronic conjunctivitis.

Vision: $R \frac{8}{9} - 1$ D. improves, $L \frac{8}{9} - 1$ D. $= \frac{8}{9}$
$R\ p = 7$ D.
$L\ p = 5.5$ D.

He converges to 9 cms. easily $\therefore c = 11$ m.a. Has been using spectacles $+ 1$ D. for work for three years. Maddox's rod test shows no latent divergence. There is *no* "insufficiency" of the internal recti, they simply suffer from natural fatigue. He is advised to go on using glasses + 1 D., but to hold his work as far (and not as *near*) away as he conveniently can. He is also advised not to work so many hours consecutively.

Muscular Asthenopia.—Myopia.

F. S., 25, clerk. Suffers from chronic conjunctivitis, which has been getting worse lately. Has myopia − 3.5 D., and he wears these glasses for distance.

His accommodation near point is 9 cms. ∴ $a = 11 - 3.5 = 7.5$ D.; his convergence near point is 18 cms. He has 1 m.a. latent divergence for distance, and 1.5 m.a. latent divergence at ¼ metre. His amplitude of convergence is 6.5 m.a. He was recommended to wear his glasses always, to keep his work at least 33 cms. off, and he returned some months later showing very great improvement, having no heterophoria for distance, and only .5 m.a. at ¼ metre.

Muscular Asthenopia.—Astigmatic Myopia.

A. E., aged 24, clerk; complains of headache and aching at back of eyes in the evening, and very often vision becomes misty, he sees double and feels dizzy; is always better on Monday, after Sunday's rest.

He has 1 m.a. of latent divergence in both eyes (not manifest); on directing him to look at the tip of a pen the eyes converge well up to 7 cms., and then the right internal rectus suddenly gives way, and the right eye turns out.

Under homatropine the shadow test shows myopic astigmatism thus:—

$$\underset{R.}{\overset{\times}{-6.5 \quad -4.5}} \qquad \underset{L.}{\overset{\times}{-4.5 \quad -6.5}}$$

and glasses—

    −6 D. sph.   −6 D. sph.
    −2 D. cyl.   −2 D. cyl.

Give $\frac{6}{9}$ in both eyes.

Out of homatropine, the same combination of glasses gives B.E. $\frac{6}{9}$, and they are ordered for distance; reading glasses are ordered with the same cylinder combined with −2 D. spherical.

As the patient is anæmic, and not at all strong, he is advised to put himself under his medical adviser, to take plenty of out-door exercise, never to bring his work nearer than *twelve inches*, and to do no near work after office hours.

He returned some months later highly delighted with the effect of his glasses. His asthenopia had disappeared, and he felt a different man.

Muscular Asthenopia, Myopia.—Insufficiency of Internal Recti.

J. F., 33, a clerk, works at bookkeeping, &c., from 10—5 every day. At night his eyes ache. Complains of double vision; he says "there is nearly always a tendency for any object to divide."

$$V < \begin{matrix} R \frac{6}{6} - 4 = \frac{6}{6} \text{ keratoscopy} = -3. \\ L \frac{6}{6} - 4 = \frac{6}{6} \quad \text{,,} \quad = -2. \end{matrix}$$
$$c\,p = 7\,D.$$

There is no manifest deviation, but static latent divergence of almost 2 m.a. is shown, and at ¼ metre he has 1 m.a.

—2 D. enables him to read well at 40 cms, and he is advised never to approach his eyes to his work nearer than this. For the present ordered distance — 4 D., reading — 2 D.

Muscular Asthenopia — convergence "insufficiency" — Myopia—Anisometropia.

F. L., age, 31, a clerk suffering from slight chronic conjunctivitis, complains of headache, chiefly frontal, coming on after work; says that lately the headache appears before he has been two hours at work.

$$V = \begin{matrix} R < \frac{6}{60} - 2.5\,D = \frac{6}{6} \\ L < \frac{6}{6} - 1\,D = \frac{6}{6} \end{matrix}$$

His convergence near point is 18 cms.; if he is told to look at the tip of a pen at this distance, and any attempt is made to bring it nearer, the right internal rectus is seen to suddenly give way, the right eye turns considerably outwards, and diplopia supervenes. Examined by the Maddox test, he shows ½ m.a. latent divergence for distance, and 1 m.a., which soon becomes 2 m.a., for ¼ metre. He was given a mixture of iron and strychnine, and advised to take a fortnight's rest, and on returning at the end of that time the following great improvement was noted, c P = 8 cms. Latent divergence for distance = ⅓ m.a., and at ¼ m. = ⅔ m.a. His range of convergence had increased from 6 m.a. to 12 m.a. !

He was advised to return to business and to use his correcting glasses for distance, and not to bring his work nearer to his eyes than 22 cms. He refused any correction of the myopia for near work.

PART IV.

RETINAL ASTHENOPIA.

RETINAL ASTHENOPIA.

Retinal Asthenopia—Torpor Retinæ.

I. PHYSIOLOGICAL CONSIDERATIONS.—Stimulation of the retina by light, produces in the optic nerve a change, similar to that which takes place in a motor nerve, when stimulated. The incidence of light on the irritable retina develops an electric change, the magnitude of which is, to a certain extent, proportionate to the intensity of the light acting as a stimulus (Foster). The vibrations of the ether are transferred by the rods and cones of the retina to the optic nerve as nervous impulses. Besides these electrical and nervous changes produced by light, we have also a photo-chemical process produced. The retinal epithelium secretes purple pigment called "visual purple," which is acted upon by light, becoming at first orange, then yellow, and finally white. This bleaching effect is produced most readily by white light.

Michael Foster says that, "Of the various prismatic rays the most active are the greenish-yellow rays, those to the blue side of these coming next, the least active being the red."[1] When the retina is stimulated by light there is (1) the effect on the visual purple or rhodopsin ; (2) the electromotive force is diminished ; (3) the processes of the hexagonal pigment cells of the retina dipping between the rods and cones are affected—they are retracted in dark-

---

[1] "Physiology," 1891, part iv., p. 1255.

ness and protruded in the light; (4) the cones also are retracted in darkness and protruded in the light (Landois and Stirling).

In the dark the visual purple is regenerated. The exact use of the visual purple is not known, but Michael Foster suggests that it may be analogous to the "sensitizer" of the photographer. What the real nature of the stimulation of the nerve-endings in the retina is we do not know, but we *do* know that the effect of this stimulation is, as in any other part of the nervous organism, associated with a liability to fatigue; and as we should expect, this fatigue of the retina is produced more quickly and with more certainty by bright white light; and ordinary stimulation, if carried to excess, or if the general nervous system is lowered, will produce the same effect.[1]

A very simple proof of fatigue of the retinal elements is the production of negative after-images. If a window be looked at for a short time and the eyes then directed to a white surface, a negative of the window is seen for a short time; the panes are dark and are intersected by white bars.

Priestley Smith says, that in neurasthenia and allied conditions of nervous prostration, peripheral anæsthesia of the retina exists, and he has so conclusively proved his point that it seems incredible that anyone, after reading his arguments, could cling to the old "central hypothesis." He further says that the peripheral anæsthesia is due to reflex contraction of the vessels which nourish the retina;[2] now this diminished blood supply to the retina renders the rods and cones very liable to exhaustion—in other words, liable to "retinal strain." This retinal strain is produced, we have seen, directly by a bright light, and just as in ciliary

---

[1] See Berry on "Subjective Symptoms in Eye Diseases," 1886, p. 19.
[2] *Oph. Rev.*, vol. iii., p. 130.

strain, we have seen that we can have direct or reflex, or both, in which latter case the direct strain need be very much less than when it acts alone, so here, when the retina is rendered liable to exhaustion by diminished blood supply, direct strain, such as the glare from snow, may produce asthenopia, whereas in a healthy condition of the retina it might have been harmless.

Not only does bright light produce nerve fatigue but at the same time it exhausts the visual purple[1] and the epithelial pigment has not time to re-secrete it.

II. SYMPTOMS OF RETINAL STRAIN.—The exhaustion of the retina may be preceded by hyper-sensitiveness, in which case pain in the eyes, or at the back of the eyes, accompanied by photophobia, will be manifested. The pain may be associated with hyperæmia, and suffusion of the eyes with tears, and may pass on to distinct conjunctivitis, or it may appear without any of these symptoms, and manifest itself simply as nerve fatigue. As in other forms of eyestrain, headache is a very common symptom, especially when hyperæsthesia precedes the anæsthesia; and bright light intensifies this headache.

Wilbrand[2] mentions *contraction of the visual field* as being one of the symptoms in neurasthenics suffering from retinal asthenopia, and Priestley Smith refers to the peculiar spiral-like chart obtained from such patients, the result of progressive exhaustion of retinal sensibility induced by prolonged visual effort. He says: "Concentric contraction of the field of vision in man is, in all cases, a sign of loss of function in the retina."[3] Nettleship says: "I am inclined to think that the only retinal affections which can at

---

[1] "Treitel on Night-Blindness," *Oph. Rev.*, vol. v., p. 173.
[2] *Ophthalmic Review*, vol. iii., p. 10.
[3] *Oph. Rev.*, vol. iii., p. 130.

present be positively set down to the effect of over-use are the temporary, though prolonged, exhaustion (torpor retinæ) which occurs in endemic night-blindness—and forms also a part of what is called snow, ice and electric light blindness, and which after all is not accompanied by any visible ophthalmoscopical changes—and the inflammatory changes which have in a few cases occurred on exposure to the intense light and heat of direct sun's rays,"[1] but suggests that some few cases may occur where excessive use of the eyes may have induced disease of the fundus, and he gives notes of eight cases of choroiditis and choroido-retinitis in which eyestrain appears to have been the cause of the disease. Brailey gives lengthy notes of a case of choroido-retinitis in the yellow spot region, in a gentleman, aged 41, which appears to have followed working at a fine pen-and-ink drawing.[2] It is certain, however, that these objective signs are rare, and more often the symptoms are purely subjective.

Night-blindness.—All healthy persons on first entering a dark room experience an inability to see, the extent of which varies with the intensity of the light they leave and the darkness of the room; in a short time physiological adaptation takes place, and objects become more and more discernible—they were temporarily " night-blind." This condition exaggerated, occurs as a symptom of retinal exhaustion due to prolonged exposure to a great glare, such as is produced by the sun shining on a large expanse of snow, chalk, sea or sand, and is specially liable to attack those who are exhausted by fatigue, or disease such as scurvy. This "idiopathic night-blindness" is unaccom-

---

[1] *Oph. Rev.*, vol. vii., p. 33.
[2] *Trans. Oph. Soc.*, vol. vii., p. 177.

panied by any retinal change, and is thus distinguished from the pathological variety; it manifests itself by a great diminution in the visual acuity, amounting often to blindness, when the light, from any cause, is reduced.

III. CAUSES OF RETINAL ASTHENOPIA:
1. From over use of the eyes.
2. From admission of too much light into the eye, due to
   (*a*) Glare of the sun, either direct or reflected. Night blindness.
   (*b*) Glare of snow (snow blindness).
   (*c*) Glare of electric light (electric light blindness).
   (*d*) Lightning.
   (*e*) Mydriasis or any cause, such as cataract operation with iridectomy, that causes the pupil to be too large (erythropsia).

These causes may be associated with:
1. A condition of health.
2. Nervo-muscular debility:
   (*a*) Neurasthenia.
   (*b*) Exhaustion from disease.
   (*c*) Reflex amblyopia,
(3. Disease of the eye.)

IV. FATIGUE OF THE RETINA FROM OVER USE.
—If this condition ever exists in the perfectly healthy it must necessarily be so masked by the symptoms of accommodative or muscular asthenopia that it would be impossible to recognise it.

But in those suffering from nervo-muscular debility it is otherwise. Neurasthenics, we have seen, show a contraction of the visual field, which is demonstrated by the spiral-like chart obtained with the perimeter, and is the result of progressive exhaustion of the retinal sensibility, induced by prolonged visual effort. There is diminished acuity of vision, and, according to Wilbrand,[1] sudden attacks of amblyopia and scotomata, and impaired memory for visual impressions, are often noticed. Among the symptoms of neurasthenic retinal asthenopia are, hyperæmia and suffusion of the eyes with tears, paresis of accommodation, photophobia and blepharospasm, after images, micropsia and monocular diplopia (Hill Griffith).

In neurasthenics, besides the actual fatigue from use of the eyes, ordinary light also produces exhaustion in many cases. It does not require any very great degree of illumination to produce this effect. An ordinary candle will do it sometimes.

Very much allied to neurasthenic amblyopia is the exhaustion of the retina occurring in those recovering from a long illness or debilitated by disease, such as anæmia; or suffering from some trouble that acts reflexly on the eyes (reflex amblyopia).

Finkelstein found that rapid exhaustibility of the retina occurred in epilepsy and hysteria, and mostly in neurasthenia; and in menstruation the central vision becomes slightly impaired, returning rapidly to the standard after the catamenia.[2]

Mooren, of Düsseldorf, and Cohn, of Breslau, refer at length to the hyperæsthesia of the retina and consequent asthenopia, that result from the reflex influence of uterine or sexual trouble. Mooren says, "We can say that any inflammatory process in any part of the genital tract, causing alterations of its shape or dimensions, can produce a hyperæsthesia of the retina. . . . When the condition lasts a long time a narrowing of the field of vision is

---

[1] *Oph. Rev.*, vol. iii., p. 45.
[2] *Oph. Rev.*, vol. vi., p. 326.

almost a constant symptom, even where there is no material diminution of sight."[1]

Ayres of Cincinnati records a few cases of anæsthesia of the retina, with contraction of the visual field associated with uterine trouble cured by strychnine injections.[2]

Priestley Smith mentions cases of ovarian disease, shock and intestinal troubles, suffering from retinal asthenopia as instances of reflex amblyopia.[3]

V. SUN BLINDNESS.—Swanzy reported two cases of central amblyopia from exposure to the direct rays of the sun. Both the patients were men, aged respectively 45 and 23, and the symptoms had appeared after looking at the sun, which was shining brightly, many times, with the eyes unprotected.

The symptoms were a central scotoma (positive) and a peculiar metamorphopsia, which consisted of a bulging or enlargement of a straight line at the point of fixation. In the first case the ophthalmoscope revealed nothing, but in the second there was a dense red spot over the macula.[4]

Deutschman, in an article on "Blinding of the Retina by direct Sunlight,"[5] gives three cases where the patients had gazed at the sun with the naked eye, and as a result acquired a central scotoma; the opthalmoscope showed a bright white spot at the centre of the macula, around which was a blood-red ring. He produced the same retinal change experimentally on rabbits; the microscope showed the change to be due to coagulation of the albumen in the tissue of the retina. The cases recovered, but not com-

---

[1] *Knapp's Arch. of Oph.*, vol. xi., p. 291.
[2] *American Journal of Oph.*, vol. ii., p. 9.
[3] *Oph. Rev.*, vol. iii., p. 130.
[4] *Oph. Rev.*, vol. ii., p. 142.
[5] *Graefe's Arch.*, bd. xxviii., 3, p. 241.

pletely. Snell gives an account of central scotoma from exposure to the direct rays of the sun in a young man aged 17, who looked through a powerful telescope during the daytime and momentarily received the full blaze of the sun's rays; and he also reports a case of *retinitis* in a girl, caused by a flash from a sun reflector.[1]

Night-Blindness.—This is specially liable to attack soldiers and sailors, especially if scurvy exists, but any debilitating influence, such as fatigue, disease, or bad food, predisposes to it. One of the best instances on record is that reported by Captain Smith, of H.M.S. "Merlin." He had command of twenty men in a Spanish privateer, and for a few days half of the men suffered from night-blindness. It was most important that all hands should be available for work day or night, and he got over the difficulty by bandaging up one eye in those that were affected, and the eye so bandaged was not affected by night-blindness, and could be used at night. [2]

Adams Frost relates two cases of "night-blindness" from exposure to bright light. Both were painters who had been engaged in painting with white colour. They had no symptoms of lead poisoning. Photophobia, pain and lachrymation were present.[3]

VI. **SNOW-BLINDNESS.**—Reich reports an epidemic of snow-blindness which occurred in 1880 in the Caucasus. There was a great glare of light produced by the rays of the sun falling on a vast stretch of snow. Among seventy well-marked cases, thirty were so severe that they were rendered for a time practically blind. Photophobia and pain were present in all, and congestion of the conjunctiva

---

[1] *Oph. Rev.*, vol. ii., p. 141.
[2] "Royal Naval Biography," vol. iv., Sept. 1801.
[3] *Trans. Oph. Soc.*, vol. v., p. 123.

in the severest cases; strong contraction of the pupils was present in all but two. Recovery was complete.[1]

Berlin says that sometimes secondary hyperæmia of the retina is observed in these cases.[2]

Graddy says that the conjunctival troubles are due to sun burn.[3]

VII. **ELECTRIC LIGHT BLINDNESS.**—The influence of electric light on the eyes is known to almost everyone. The small lamps containing an incandescent wire, used in house illumination, are comparatively harmless, but the intensely bright arc light, if unprotected, sometimes produces very severe effects.

The excessive stimulation of the retina produces scotomata and after-images, accompanied by pain, photophobia and conjunctivitis (Felix Terrier[4]). Widmarck, by experiments upon rabbits has proved that this action is caused by the chemical (ultra violet) rays, whereas Martin says the affection is produced by the light rays, as in sun and snow-blindness.[5] When the cause is removed the effect soon disappears, although in a case reported by Little, impairment of vision and haziness round the disc lasted for two months.[6]

Maklakoff believes the symptoms produced by electric light are due to hyperæsthesia of the eyes (and skin) struck by the light, combined with hyperæmia and œdema, which are produced by the chemical action of the rays of light.[7]

Rockliffe describes a case of acute conjunctivitis due to

---

[1] *Oph. Rev.*, vol. ii., p. 109.
[2] *Knapp's Arch. of Oph.*, vol. xix., p. 101.
[3] *Knapp's Arch. of Oph.*, vol. xviii., p. 119.
[4] *Archives d'oph.*, vol. viii., p. 1.
[5] *Knapp's Arch.*, vol. xviii., p. 108.
[6] *Oph. Rev.*, vol. ii., p. 196.
[7] *Arch. d'oph.*, vol. ix., p. 97.

the action of electric light; the patient had adjusted the carbon points of an electric lamp of 3,000 candle power. Lachrymation, photophobia, pain and swelling were present. Recovery was complete.[1]

Emrys-Jones in a paper on "The Effects of Electric Light on the Eye,"[2] gives a very full report of a case of "electric light" strain. The light was an arc light of 2,000 candle power, and the patient said that gazing for one minute at the light from eighteen to twenty-four inches off, produced "certain inflammation." He found that an excess of current that gave a violet light, or a defect of current that gave an orange light, was less injurious than the normal white light. Unpleasant after-images resulted which lasted according to the amount of the strain, and if the latter was strong enough, inflammation set in, in from six to nine hours. Pain, as if dust was in the eyes, lachrymation, photophobia and dilatation of the pupil followed, and when the inflammation subsided the eyes were very sore, tender and intolerant of light.

Ljubinski calls the affection "ophthalmia photo electrica," and says that the continued effect of the electric light causes photophobia, lachrymation and pain, most manifest at night, with hyperæmia of the optic nerve.[3]

Gould believes that the injurious effects of electric light when they exist are due to the intensity, and not to the preponderance of the ultra-violet rays.[4]

Case: *Retinal Asthenopia.—Electric Light.*

E. K., age 28, clerk, works all day close to a strong electric light (arc); complains of intense aching and blurring of the eyes in the evening.

---

[1] *Oph. Rev.*, vol. i., p. 308.
[2] *Oph. Rev.*, vol ii., p. 106.
[3] *Centralbl. f. prakt. Augenhk.*, 1889, p. 176.
[4] *Knapp's Arch. of Oph.*, vol. xviii., p. 495.

$$V = \begin{matrix} R. \\ L. \end{matrix} < \begin{matrix} \frac{6}{9} \\ \frac{6}{9} \end{matrix} > -.5 \text{ D. slightly improved.}$$

He has 9 D. of accommodation power, and 9 m.a. of convergence. Marked conjunctivitis in both eyes. Rest to the eyes and boracic lotion effected a cure.

VIII. **LIGHTNING BLINDNESS.**—Leber mentions transient loss of sight, with contraction of the field of vision as sometimes resulting from a lightning stroke.[1]

Von Graefe reports a case in which hyperæsthesia was present, with concentric limitation of the field in one eye, and facial spasm on the same side.

IX. **ERYTHROPSIA.**—Under the heading of erythropsia or red vision, Dufour reports four cases. Three of the patients had undergone an operation for cataract, and the fourth had had large iridectomies performed. The erythropsia appeared in the evening of a bright day after a fall of snow, and lasted till noon of the next day. Eserine, by contracting the pupils, diminished or removed the symptoms, and objects looked at appeared violet, pink or red.[2] Dobrowolsky produced this condition artificially by dilating the pupil and gazing at a bright cloud near the sun or the edge of the sun itself.[3] Most recent writers agree that this condition is due to fatigue of the retinal elements that perceive blue and violet (Szili). It is very often connected with general nerve exhaustion.

Kubli[4] records four cases of erythropsia, one after cataract extraction with a broad iridectomy, and two associated with night-blindness. He thinks this association with night-blindness indicates that the phenomenon is of *retinal* origin.

---

[1] *Oph. Rev.*, vol. ii., p. 146.
[2] *Annales d'Ocul.*, vol. 99, p. 135.
[3] *Oph. Rev.*, vol. vii., p. 219.
[4] *Knapp's Arch.*, vol. xvii., p. 125.

X. TREATMENT.—The treatment in retinal asthenopia is simple, and the cure generally complete unless complications exist, as in the neurasthenic and reflex form.

Complete rest to the eyes in a darkened room allows the visual purple to be re-secreted, and very soon removes night blindness. The general health should be attended to, and aperients administered; tonics, such as iron and strychnine, are often useful. When local symptoms exist, such as conjunctivitis and pain, &c., warm fomentations of opium, and, if necessary, leeches to the temple may be resorted to.

In snow-blindness, rubbing the eyes with snow is the measure usually adopted. Neurasthentic retinal asthenopia is very often a most obstinate complaint; the treatment of course consists in removing, if possible, the neurasthenic condition. Tinted glasses should not be given to these patients, because they only tend to increase the hypersensitiveness of the retina.

In reflex amblyopia, if no organic change has taken place, the symptoms generally disappear when the cause is removed.

If electric light asthenopia is present, cocaine, with cold applications locally, and chloral internally, should be prescribed (Ljubinski).

As prevention is better than cure, those whose eyes are exposed to glare, should have them protected by gauze, or tinted spectacles; workmen exposed to electric light should have compound red and green spectacles or dark grey glasses (Ljubinski).

NOTE.

The accurate centering of Glasses.

To really accurately fit, every spectacle frame should be *made for the patient*, and this should be done in every case where the pocket allows it. The centre of the glass should coincide with the visual axis. Distance glasses and those which are ordered to be worn always, should be centered for distance; working or reading glasses should be centered for the working or reading distance. We have seen that glasses have a prismatic effect if decentered. A convex glass may be said to consist of two prisms with the bases in contact. If the glasses, are too wide apart the patient looks through the inner side of the glass, which has the same effect as looking through a prism with its base outwards, consequently the convergence effort will have to be increased. If the glasses are too close together, we have the same effect as a prism with its base inwards, and the convergence effort will be diminished, the accommodation being in excess. Concave glasses may be said to be two prisms with their apices in contact, and the effect of their being out of the centre is the reverse of that of convex lenses. When these results are not desired, that is, when the lenses are not purposely decentered, it is easy to understand how a badly-fitting spectacle can undo our work.

Ward Holden[1] suggests that the best method of testing whether glasses are properly centered, is to alternately cover each eye, and by that means detect any deviation, directing the patient to fix for distance if for distance glasses, and at the reading distance for reading glasses. If deviation exists, find the prism that will prevent it, and by the formula (see page 140), calculate the displacement

---

[1] *Knapp's Arch.*, vol xx., p. 24.

necessary, dividing the effect equally between the two eyes. For instance, if the prism that corrects the deviation is 2° base in, and the lenses are $+$ 3D, we have $8.7 \times 2 \div 3 = 5.8$ mm. so that each lens will have to be shifted 2.9 mm. inwards. If the lenses were purposely decentered to correct insufficiency of the external or internal rectus muscles, we apply the same test, and if deviation exists, ascertain by prisms base in or out whether the decentering is too much or too little.

The plane of the glasses should be perpendicular to the visual axis when in use, hence reading glasses should be inclined from the vertical, the upper end being tilted forward.

The glasses should be so fitted that they are as near as possible to the eyes, and yet not near enough for the lashes to touch them. Concave glasses are weakened, and convex glasses strengthened, by removing them from the eye, and *vice versâ*.

Jackson has pointed out that a cylindrical lens becomes more cylindrical, and a spherical one sphero-cylindrical, by being placed obliquely before the eyes.[1]

The bridge of the frames should fit the nose well, and not be liable to slip down. It is always best to have spectacles and not folders—folders never fit; nevertheless they are very useful to the presbyope, and the myope may be allowed to use them; but under *no* circumstances should they be given to young people or to astigmatics. The so-called "astigmatic *pince-nez*," which do not fold, and work with a horizontal spring, may be allowed in astigmatism, but are inferior to spectacles. Except in the case of monocular amblyopia beyond any hope of cure, or monocular blindness, single eyeglasses should be strictly forbidden.

---

[1] *Oph. Rev.*, vol. vi., p. 247.

APPENDIX.

THE ASSOCIATION OF BLEPHARITIS AND AMETROPIA WITH ANALYSIS OF ONE HUNDRED CASES.[1]

Since Roosa first drew attention to the association of blepharitis with ametropia, Hall in 1882[2] has published a list of ten cases of blepharitis, in nine of whom ametropia was found to exist, but since then no further statistics have been published. Blepharitis is usually divided into two varieties: (1) the non-ulcerative and (2) the ulcerative; they merge the one into the other, and the ulceration is nature's effort to get rid of the scabs which form from the increased secretion of the glands. The form of the disease I would specially refer to is the chronic mild blepharitis beginning in early childhood, and sometimes continuing through life when untreated. Careful examination shows that in these cases the disease is practically limited to the facial margin of the free border of the lids, *i.e.*, the most immediate region of the lashes. The skin is here slightly congested, and is covered by thin fine scales, often very small. These "weak eyes," as they are termed, are a constant source of trouble to the patient, for the slightest irritation, such as dust or smoke, causes a spreading of the inflammation to the conjunctiva.

---

[1] Read at the Annual Meeting of the B.M.A., 1894.
[2] *New York Medical Record*, April, 1882.

The worst form of blepharitis, so common among the children of the poor, called *eczema tarsi* or *sycosis*, often begins with an attack of phlyctenular ophthalmia; the patients are generally strumous and dirty, which conditions are often considered to be the real cause of the disease, but all such cases I have examined were ametropic, and although the constitutional tendency to eczema, &c., and the uncleanliness may materially "feed" the disease, I believe the asthenopia causes the eyes to be attacked in the first instance.

Analysis of the 100 *cases.*—Cases not picked. In all, the disease had lasted over a year, in many, all the life. They were all placed under the influence of a mydriatic. Atropine was used for those under 20, and homatropine and cocaine for those over 20.

Taking ametropia to signify a refraction of more than a quarter of a dioptre of astigmatism, any myopia, and more than one dioptre of hypermetropia, *i.e.*, taking it in its broadest sense, every one of the 100 patients was ametropic.

Refraction of the 200 *Eyes.*

Hypermetropia	64
Hypermetropic astigmatism	96
Mixed astigmatism	8
Myopia	5
Myopic astigmatism	26
Emmetropia	1
	200

Note that in 168 eyes (*i.e.*, 84 per cent.) hypermetropia existed in some form. Out of the 200 eyes 194 were either hypermetropic or astigmatic (giving rise to *accommodative asthenopia*). The two cases of myopia in both eyes (7 and 39) had inefficiency of the internal recti (causing *muscular asthenopia*). Forty-one of the patients were anisometropic. In most of the cases the ametropia was of low degree, and out of the 96 eyes in which hypermetropic astigmatism existed, the astigmatism in 72 was not more than ·5D. This is exactly as one would expect it to be; it is just this low form of astigmatism which is most productive of asthenopia.

Sex.—Thirty-five were males and sixty-five females.

Age.—The average age was 17 years.

Occupation.—Sixty-seven of the patients were engaged at near work during most of the day. Forty-four were school children.

Vision before testing.—Eighty-seven of the patients sought advice for "sore eyes" and were unconscious of any defect of vision, and of these sixty-six had with one or both eyes V. = $\frac{6}{9}$ or better, and fifty-two had V. = $\frac{6}{6}$ or better.

To sum up: (1) Blepharitis is essentially a disease of youth, and when we find it present in older patients, it has existed since youth. (2) It is an expression of asthenopia, the result of ametropia, which is invariably present. Just as asthenopia shows itself as headache or ocular pain in those whose nervous system is so constituted, so in others, especially strumous patients and those who exhibit a tendency to eczema, does asthenopia mark its presence by blepharitis.

It may be contended by some that 100 normal patients with no blepharitis would have shown the same percentage of ametropia, but this is not so. Work Dodd[1] in his list of fifty people apparently normal, whose refraction was

---

[1] *Trans. Oph. Soc.*, vol. xiii., p. 208.

examined, gives out of the 100 eyes twenty emmetropic in the sense I use them above, *i.e.*, 20 per cent.

In my list of 200 eyes the proportion of emmetropia was much lower; but even if this were not so, if all eyes were more or less ametropic, my answer is, the proof that asthenopia causes the blepharitis lies in the undisputed fact that case after case which has resisted treatment for years has yielded when the ametropia was corrected, and the patient given glasses to wear constantly; this is the essential part of the *treatment* of blepharitis, namely, to paralyse the accommodation, find the refractive error, and order suitable spectacles. The local application of mild astringent lotions and ointment should be employed of course, and in severe cases epilation and painting with nitrate of silver may have to be resorted to, but no permanent cure can be hoped for until the eye-strain has been removed.

ONE HUNDRED CASES OF BLEPHARITIS.

No.	Sex.	Age.	Occupation.	Vision.	R. Refraction under a Mydriatic. L.
1	M	38	Hair dresser		+ 1 cy. ob. — 1·5 cy. ob.
2	M	14	School		+ 1·5 B.E.
3	F	19	Servant		+ 3 B.E.
4	M	33	Compositor		—·5 cy. vert. { + 4 / + 1 cy. hor.
5	M	23	No occupation		+ 3 + 2
6	M	22	Piano tuner		{ + 4·5 / + 1·5 cy. ob. { + 3·5 / + 4 cy. vert.
7	F	15	School		— 2 B.E.
8	F	18	At home		+ 3·5 + 2·5
9	F	16	Teacher		+ 1 . { + 1 / +·5 cy. hor.
10	F	19	Clerk		+·5 cy. hor. B.E.
11	M	11	School		+ 2 B.E.
12	F	18	Dressmaker		+·5 cy. vert. B.E.
13	F	4	...		+ 4 B.E.
14	F	17	Dressmaker		+ 2·5 B.E.
15	F	6	School		+ 2 { + 2 / + 1 cy. vert.
16	M	23	Printer		{ + 2·5 / +·5 cy. ob. { + 1 / +·75 cy. vert.
17	F	30	Shop assistant		{ — 1 / —·5 cy. hor. B.E.
18	F	42	Housewife		+ 3·5 B.E.
19	F	19	Packer		+ 5 { + 4·5 / +·75 cy. vert.
20	F	13	School		+·5 cy. hor. B.E.

APPENDIX.

One Hundred Cases of Blepharitis.—*continued*.

No.	Sex.	Age.	Occupation.	Vision.	R. Refraction under a Mydriatic. L.
21	M	22	Carpenter	$\frac{6}{9}$	$\{+ 1\cdot 5$ $+ 1\cdot 5$ $\{+ \cdot 5$ cy. ob.
22	F	15	At home	$\frac{6}{12}$	$+ 3$ $\{+ 3$ $\{+ \cdot 5$ cy. vert.
23	F	22	Tie maker	$\frac{6}{6}$	$\{+ 1$ $\{+ 2$ $\{+ \cdot 5$ cy. vert. $\{+ \cdot 5$ cy. vert.
24	F	14	School	$\frac{6}{6}$	$\{+ 1\cdot 5$ $\{+ 5$ cy. vert. B.E.
25	F	45	Nurse	$\frac{6}{9}$	$+ 1$ $+ 2$
26	M	37	Compositor	$\frac{6}{9}$	$+ 3$ $+ 4$
27	M	9	School	$\frac{6}{12}$	$\{+ 1$ $\{+ 1$ cy. ob. $+ 4$
28	M	19	Clerk	$\frac{6}{9}$	$+ 4$ $+ 5\cdot 5$
29	F	15	School	$\frac{6}{6}$	$\{+ \cdot 5$ $\{+ \cdot 5$ $\{+ \cdot 25$ cy. hor. $\{+ \cdot 25$ cy. hor.
30	F	22	Servant	$<\frac{6}{60}$	$\{- 6$ $\{- 6$ $\{- 2$ cy. hor. $\{- 1$ cy. vert.
31	F	30	Housewife	$\frac{6}{6}$	$\{+ \cdot 75$ cy. vert. B.E. $\{- \cdot 5$
32	M	9	School	$\frac{6}{6}$	$\{+ 1$ cy. ob. $\{+ 1$ cy. ob. $\{+ 1$ $\{+ 1$
33	M	8	,,	?	$+ 4$ cy. vert. $+ 3$ cy. vert.
34	M	27	Lawyer	$\frac{6}{6}$	$\{+ \cdot 5$ cy. ob. $\{+ 5$ cy. ob. $\{- \cdot 25$ $\{- \cdot 25$
35	F	12	School	$\frac{6}{5}$	$+ 3\cdot 5$ B.E.
36	M	20	College	$\frac{6}{6}$	$+ \cdot 5$ cy. vert. $+ \cdot 5$
37	F	11	School	$\frac{6}{9}$	$+ 2\cdot 5$ B.E.
38	F	21	Housewife	$\leq \frac{6}{60}$	$\{- 18$ $\}- 7$ $\}$ 2 m.a. $\{- 2$ cy. vert. $\}- \cdot 75$ cy. ob. $\}$ lat. div.
39	M	30	Doctor	$<\frac{6}{60}$	$- 6$ $- 5\cdot 5$, 1 m.a. lat. div.
40	M	10	School	$\frac{6}{6}$	$+ \cdot 5$ cy. vert. B.E.
41	F	25	Music teacher	$\frac{6}{9}$	$\{+ \cdot 25$ $+ \cdot 5$ cy. ob. $\{+ \cdot 25$ cy. ob.
42	F	17	School	$\frac{6}{6}$	$+ \cdot 5$ cy. hor. B.E.
43	F	25	Music teacher	$\frac{6}{5}$	$+ \cdot 5$ cy. ob. $+ \cdot 5$ cy. ob.
44	M	9	School	$\frac{6}{6}$	$\{+ 1$ $\{+ 1$ $\{+ \cdot 5$ cy. vert. $\{+ \cdot 5$ cy. vert.
45	F	10	,,	$\frac{6}{7}$	$+ \cdot 75$ cy. vert. B.E.
46	F	30	Housewife	$\frac{6}{12}$	$\{- \cdot 5$ cy. ob. $\{- \cdot 75$ cy. hor. $\{- \cdot 5$ $\{- \cdot 5$
47	F	15	School	?	$-3\cdot 5$ $\{- 3$ $\{- \cdot 5$ cy. vert.
48	F	30	Lady nurse	$\frac{6}{6}$	$\{+ \cdot 5$ B.E. $\{+ \cdot 5$ cy. vert.
49	F	21	Book folder	$\frac{6}{6}$	$+ 1\cdot 75$ B.E.
50	F	13	School	$\frac{6}{6}$	$\{+ \cdot 5$ $\{+ \cdot 5$ $\{+ \cdot 5$ cy. ob. $\{+ \cdot 5$ cy. ob.
51	F	23	Ward maid	$\frac{6}{9}$	$+ 3\cdot 5$ B.E.
52	F	15	School	?	$+ 4\cdot 5$ B.E.

ONE HUNDRED CASES OF BLEPHARITIS.—*continued.*

No.	Sex.	Age.	Occupation.	Vision.	R. Refraction under a Mydriatic. L.
53	M	11	School.	$\frac{6}{6}$	$\begin{cases} +\cdot 5 \\ +\cdot 5 \text{ cy. vert.} \end{cases}$ B.E.
54	F	9	,,	$\frac{6}{18}$	$\begin{cases} -\cdot 5 \\ -2\cdot 5 \text{ cy. hor.} \end{cases}$ B.E.
55	F	19	Corset maker	$\frac{6}{12}$	$+\cdot 75$ cy. vert. $+1\cdot 5$ cy. ob.
56	F	10	School	$\frac{6}{36}$	$\begin{cases} -1 \\ -3 \text{ cy. hor.} \end{cases}$ B.E.
57	F	20	At home	$\frac{6}{6}$	$\begin{cases} +\cdot 5 \\ +\cdot 75 \text{ cy. vert.} \end{cases}$ $\begin{cases} -1\cdot 5 \\ +\cdot 75 \text{ cy. vert.} \end{cases}$
58	F	13	School	$\frac{6}{18}$	$+1\cdot 5$ cy. vert. B.E.
59	M	7	,,	?	$\begin{cases} +2 \\ +1 \text{ cy. vert.} \end{cases}$ $\begin{cases} +2\cdot 5 \\ +1\cdot 5 \text{ cy. vert.} \end{cases}$
60	M	17	Clerk	?	$\begin{cases} -4 \\ -1 \text{ cy. ob.} \end{cases}$ $\begin{cases} -4 \\ -1 \text{ cy. ob.} \end{cases}$
61	F	19	At home	$\frac{6}{12}$	$\begin{cases} -1\cdot 5 \text{ cy. vert.} \\ -1\cdot 5 \end{cases}$ $-1\cdot 5$ cy. ob.
62	M	13	School	$\frac{6}{6}$	$+1\cdot 5$ cy. vert. B.E.
63	F	16	Shop assistant	$\frac{6}{6}$	$+\cdot 5$ cy. vert. B.E.
64	F	12	School	$\frac{6}{7}$	$\begin{cases} +1\cdot 25 \\ +\cdot 75 \text{ cy. vert.} \end{cases}$ B.E.
65	M	11	,,	$\frac{6}{6}$	$\begin{cases} +\cdot 5 \text{ cy. ob.} \\ +1\cdot 5 \end{cases}$
66	M	11½	,,	$\frac{6}{12}$	$+3$ $+\cdot 5$ $+3\cdot 5$
67	F	26	At home	$\frac{6}{12}$	$\begin{cases} +3 \\ +1 \text{ cy. vert.} \end{cases}$ $\begin{cases} +3 \\ \cdot 5 \text{ cy. vert.} \end{cases}$
68	F	31	,,	$<\frac{6}{60}$	$\begin{cases} -2 \\ -4 \text{ cy. ob.} \end{cases}$ $\begin{cases} -2 \\ -5 \text{ cy. ob.} \end{cases}$
69	M	2½	...	?	$+4\cdot 5$ B.E.
70	M	5½	School	$\frac{6}{6}$	$+2\cdot 5$ B.E.
71	F	20	Ward maid	$\frac{6}{24}$	$\begin{cases} +\cdot 5 \text{ cy. vert.} \\ +1 \end{cases}$ B.E.
72	M	5	School	?	$+3$ B.E.
73	M	12	,,	$\frac{6}{6}$	$+2$ $+1\cdot 5$
74	F	38	Housewife	$\frac{6}{18}$	$\begin{cases} -\cdot 5 \\ -\cdot 5 \text{ cy. hor.} \end{cases}$ $\begin{cases} -1 \\ -\cdot 5 \text{ cy. hor.} \end{cases}$
75	F	29	Parlour maid	$\frac{6}{6}$	$\begin{cases} +\cdot 25 \\ +\cdot 5 \text{ cy. vert.} \end{cases}$ $+\cdot 25$
76	F	3	...	?	$+3$ $+2$
77	F	10	School	$\frac{6}{18}$	$\begin{cases} +\cdot 25 \\ +\cdot 5 \text{ cy. vert.} \end{cases}$ $\begin{cases} +\cdot 5 \\ +\cdot 5 \text{ cy. vert.} \end{cases}$
78	M	17	Errand boy	$\frac{6}{12}$	$\begin{cases} +1 \\ +\cdot 5 \text{ cy. vert.} \end{cases}$ $\begin{cases} +1 \\ +\cdot 5 \text{ cy. vert.} \end{cases}$
79	F	10	School	$\frac{6}{9}$	$+2\cdot 5$ B.E.
80	F	16	At home	$\frac{6}{12}$	$\begin{cases} +\cdot 25 \text{ cy. hor.} \\ +\cdot 5 \end{cases}$ B.E.
81	M	9	School	$\frac{6}{18}$	$\begin{cases} +1 \\ -4 \text{ cy. hor.} \end{cases}$ $\begin{cases} +2 \\ -4 \text{ cy. hor.} \end{cases}$
82	F	18	Packer	$\frac{6}{12}$	$+2$ $+3$ $+2\cdot 5$ cy. ob. $+\cdot 75$ cy. vert.
83	F	11	School	$\frac{6}{18}$	$+\cdot 25$ cy. vert. $+2$ cy. ob.
84	F	22	Dressmaker	$\frac{6}{24}$	$+1\cdot 5$ cy. vert. $+1$ cy. vert.

ONE HUNDRED CASES OF BLEPHARITIS.—*continued.*

No.	Sex.	Age.	Occupation.	Vision.	R. Refraction under a Mydriatic. L.	
85	M	23	Shopman	$\frac{6}{6}$	+ 2·5	+ 4·5
86	F	14	School	$\frac{6}{6}$	{ +·5 +·5 cy. vert.	— 2 cy. hor. B.E.
87	F	13	,,	$\frac{6}{6}$	+·5 — 1 cy. hor.	
88	M	14	,,	$\frac{6}{6}$	— 2 — 1 cy. vert.	+·5 cy. vert.
89	F	18	,,	$\frac{6}{5}$	+·5 cy. ob.	Em.
90	M	8	,,	$\frac{6}{9}$	+ 3·5	+ 3
91	F	21	At home	$\frac{6}{6}$	+·5 cy. ob.	+·5 cy. ob.
92	M	14	School	$\frac{6}{5}$	+·5 cy. ob.	+·5 cy. ob.
93	M	26	Doctor	$\frac{6}{9}$	{ +·5 +·5 cy. vert.	+·5
94	M	12	School	$\frac{6}{5}$	+·25	+·5 cy. vert.
95	F	11	,,	$\frac{6}{5}$	+ 3·5	+ 1·5
96	F	26	At home	$\frac{6}{5}$	{ +·5 +·5 cy. vert.	+·5 cy. vert.
97	F	20	,,	$\frac{6}{4}$	+3·5	{ + 3 +·5 cy. vert.
98	F	23	,,	$\frac{6}{6}$	{ + 1 cy. vert. — 1	{ — 1 cy. ob. — 1
99	F	20	,,	$\frac{6}{5}$	{ +·5 +·5 cy. vert. B.E.	+ 1 cy. vert.
100	F	10	School	$\frac{6}{6}$	{ +·5 +·5 cy. vert.	

ABBREVIATIONS.

Cy. = cylinder; vert. = vertical axis; hor. = horizontal axis; ob. = oblique axis; lat. div. = latent divergence. The numbers are dioptres, and, except when otherwise stated, refer to spherical lenses.

ON THE VARIOUS MANIFESTATIONS OF EYE-STRAIN UPON THE EYE ITSELF AND THE BEARING THIS HAS UPON TREATMENT.[1]

Presidential Address delivered before the West Kent Medico-Chirurgical Society, May 1, 1896.

I shall not refer here to ocular pain, headache, and the remoter effects of eyestrain. These I and others have dealt with elsewhere, and they are more or less known to all of you. In passing I would briefly call your attention to a paper I read before the British Medical Association[2] two years ago, in which I showed that *blepharitis* was invariably associated with an error of refraction, and that 65 per cent. of the cases were astigmatic. A longer experience has only served to confirm the views expressed in that paper, and I consider that the treatment (although not the only treatment) for blepharitis is the proper correction of the error of refraction and the wearing of glasses. Now here, as all through my paper, I do not want you to understand that I consider eyestrain to be the only cause of blepharitis. A strumous diathesis, dirt, and many other causes may exist, but the eyestrain, I maintain, is the cause that determines the attack on the eye or on the

---

[1] Reprinted from the *Transactions of the West Kent Medico-Chirurgical Society*, 1896.
[2] *Ophthalmological Review*, November, 1894.

eyelid. You may cure the disease for a time by active local and general treatment, but if the strain is not removed you will sooner or later have a recurrence.

Conjunctivitis.—We may divide this disease into five groups :—

1. *Purulent Conjunctivitis* (gonorrhœal or ophthalmia neanatorum.)
2. *Muco-purulent* (catarrhal ophthalmia, spring catarrh, &c.).
3. *Granular* (trachoma, follicular conj., granular ophthalmia).
4. *Phlyctenular.*
5. *Diphtheritic.*

Only in the phlyctenular variety do I suggest that there is any marked association with ametropia, but in other forms, which have become chronic and resist treatment, I strongly advocate that the refraction should be tested, and if any refractive error be discovered it should be corrected. I am confident that you will then find the disease much more amenable to local and general treatment.

Keratitis.—You know how frequently children suffer from phlyctenular keratitis. A phlyctenule forms in the middle of the cornea, more often than not *over* the pupil; this breaks down and an ulcer results, photophobia is intense, the ulcer is neglected, and a general keratitis ensues, and when, finally, the disease is cured (?) a dense corneal opacity is left as a scar that interferes with vision for ever afterwards. You know how useful atropine is in such cases, and how, if properly put into the eye, the child will in a few days be able to open its eye, and in a very short time be well. Why is atropine such a useful agent? *Because it puts the eye at rest.* Follow the history of that child. The eye gets well, you cease using the atropine, and all goes on well for some time; in the course of, say, a year or longer it has an attack of measles, or in some way the system gets lowered, and the child is brought to you again. I have scores and scores of old hospital letters with the records of such cases. A year's interval and then the word *relapse* occurs on the patient's letter; a few weeks of treatment and the patient gets well, another interval, and another *relapse*; and so on. When the child is well, and before ceasing the atropine, test the refraction: you will find an error, and in most cases a considerable amount of *astigmatism*. Put that child into glasses and you prevent the relapse. I think the eyestrain determines the attack on the eye, say, in a strumous child, and one recovering from an illness in exactly the same way that an unhealthy joint will determine an attack of gout in it. When we realise the enormous number of people whose vision is permanently lowered through these scars, the result of, in many cases, recurrent corneal ulcers, we cannot help feeling that the old adage, "Prevention is better than cure," was never better applied.

Scleritis.—Inflammation of the sclerotic is in many cases a very painful complaint, it is exceedingly obstinate, and sometimes appears quite unamenable to treatment. It is associated very often with the rheumatic diathesis. Leeches, blisters, atropine, fomentations and internal exhibition of salicine may ameliorate matters, and the disease settles down into a chronic or subacute state, or may get well only to reappear again some time later. In a large percentage of cases that have been under my care during the last few years I have found a marked error of refraction, and on correcting this with glasses the various remedies have acted like a charm. Some cases that have resisted treatment for months have been cured in a week or ten days.

Iritis.—The intimate association of the iris with the ciliary body and muscle would lead us to expect that strain would have a perceptible effect on the causation or aggravation of this disease; and so it has. It is in *recurrent iritis* that I would specially draw your attention to this association. You know what an annoying disease *recurrent iritis* is, how it recurs in one or both eyes, or alternately, year after year, or with longer or shorter intervals, and how, from the deposit of lymph and pigment on the anterior capsule, or from the delay of treatment with atropine, from the adhesions formed, the eye is left worse off after each attack. You know that the treatment has been *iridectomy*; but an operation is always looked upon as a very serious thing, and it is, in fact, a serious matter, but the worst is that iridectomy does not always prevent a recurrence. During the last three years I have attempted to determine the refraction of every iritis, and where I succeeded I have found in every case a serious error, and I believe the first, if not the best treatment for *recurrent iritis*, is the correction of refractive errors. In this way I have, in many instances, prevented a relapse in patients who were constantly suffering.

Glaucoma.—The fluid secreted by the glands of the ciliary body nourishes the various structures in the eye, notably the vitreous and lens, and the greater part of the fluid passes from the posterior chamber through the pupil into the anterior chamber, and thence out at the filtration angle into the choroidal veins. The tension of the eye is raised by increase of this fluid in the eye, either (1) by its hypersecretion, or (2) its obstructed exit at the filtration angle due to its increased viscidity or to actual obstruction at this spot, or both, and we get glaucoma. Now, irritation of the fifth nerve and dilatation of the ciliary vessels will cause hypersecretion, and although Priestley Smith says "the hypothesis that glaucoma is the expression of a persistent hypersecretion remains a hypothesis,"[1] still I want you to bear in mind that it is a hypothesis, and withal a very reasonable one.

But let us pass on to the real cause of primary glaucoma —obstructed excretion. We find, according to Priestley Smith, three important facts:[2]—

(1) The size of the lens increases throughout life, and the liability to glaucoma increases throughout life.

(2) The liability to primary glaucoma is greatest in exceptionally *small* eyes.

(3) Hypermetropia is the commonest refractive state in eyes affected with primary glaucoma.

All these three factors tend to block the filtration angle.

Now, with reference to hypermetropia, I want you to recognise three important facts:—

(1) The ciliary muscle is always enlarged in hypermetropia, and with it very often the ciliary body is also hypertrophied; this tends, of course, to obstruct the filtration angle, and might also lead to hypersecretion.

(2) Hypermetropia uncorrected always means considerable eyestrain, because the eye is never at rest, except during sleep.

(3) Hypermetropia in a large number of cases is associated with astigmatism, which would, of course, increase the strain.

Walker (*Trans. of Int. Med. Congress*, 1881) and Shoen (*Trans. Int. Oph. Congress*, 1888) both put forth the con-

---

[1] "Glaucoma," 1891, p. 39.   [2] *Ibid.*, p. 84.

tention that hypermetropia might probably start glaucoma through the excessive strain in the accommodation, but Priestley Smith answered this by asserting that, according to his tables, the liability to glaucoma is greatest at a time of life when the accommodation is in abeyance. My answer to this is that by his own tables he shows that, although the liability reaches its maximum at 60, it begins to rise rapidly after 30, and that its most rapid rise is about 40, just at the period when the accommodation may be taxed to its utmost, and certainly is not in abeyance. Again, as I have said, astigmatism is in a large number of cases associated with hypermetropia, and this of itself must, if uncorrected, cause strain.

I have several patients under my care who have had one slight attack of primary glaucoma, and who, by wearing correcting lenses, have succeeded in warding off another attack; this may be a coincidence, but if it is it appears to me to be a very remarkable one. Please quite understand me. I do not suggest for a moment that every case of glaucoma is due to eyestrain; but I do maintain that from what we know of eyestrain it is highly probable that, given other conditions, it may start an attack, and thus form an important factor in the causation of this dire disease.

Cataract.—Although for some time past I have fully recognised the important part that *astigmatism* plays in the causation of cataract, I confess I was very surprised at the result of the investigation I made for this paper. I have taken 200 cases of cataract eyes from my private case-books, beginning with my last cataract patient and ceasing when I reached the two-hundredth. In a large number of these cases the cataract was incipient and often only discovered when the pupil was dilated, and consequently the patient had no idea of the presence of the disease.

I have only considered such cases as cataract when the lens showed opaque striæ or patches in its substance, and have excluded all cases of opacities on the capsule the result of inflammation. In almost all the cases the examination was made, and the refraction worked out under homatropine. Those cases in which the density of the cataract prevented the estimation of the refraction were excluded. Counting an error of refraction to be any astigmatism over ·25 D., any hypermetropia over 1 D., and any myopia, I found ametropia present in every case, and astigmatism present in 150, *i.e.*, 75 per cent.

The refraction of 200 cataracts.

Astigmatism.
Hypermetropia	... ...	48
„ c. presbyopia	...	17
Myopia	...	64
„ c. presbyopia	...	15
Mixed	...	3
„ c. presbyopia	...	3
		150

Hypermetropia.
Simple	...	4
„ c. presbyopia	...	16
		20

Myopia.
Simple	...	14
„ c. presbyopia	...	13
		27

Presbyopia.
Simple	...	3
		200

Astigmatism present in 75 per cent.

What is the percentage of astigmatism present in all eyes? Work Dodd[1] found on examining fifty people with apparently normal sight that 9 of them, *i.e.*, 18 per cent., were astigmatic. Contrast this 18 per cent. with 75 per cent. shown in the above table, and surely these figures indicate a distinct association between astigmatism and cataract.

If astigmatism may lead to cataract you may very well ask what is the *modus operandi* ?

With few exceptions the seat of regular astigmatism is in the cornea, due to a difference in the curvature of the different meridians; added to this there is sometimes found a "static crystalline astigmatism," due to a difference in the curvature of the different meridians of the lens, and the two together make up the total astigmatism of the eye which is revealed under an ordinary examination. But most frequently, although astigmatism of the eye is suspected, where it is of low degree it may be impossible to detect it without resorting to a mydriatic. Donders, in 1864, first drew attention to this, and he pointed out that the corneal astigmatism was masked and corrected by an inverse astigmatism of the lens. Dobrowalsky, in 1868, asserted that the crystalline astigmatism was produced by an unequal contraction of the ciliary muscle, and Hensen and Voelckers later have shown by experiments upon animals that this unequal contraction is possible. They showed that when a filament of the ciliary nerve was divided the portion of the muscle supplied by it was relaxed, and that on stimulating the cut end a local contraction took place.

But, quite apart from the physiological proof, the clinical

---

[1] *Trans. Ophth. Society*, vol. xiii., p. 208.

proofs are, to my mind, so perfectly conclusive that, in spite of the fact that many ophthalmologists decline to accept this theory, I myself thoroughly believe it.

Let me take a typical case. A patient complains of headache accentuated by near work. Examination reveals no refractive error. The ciliary muscle is paralysed by a mydriatic, and astigmatism is discovered. This is corrected by cylinders, the glasses are ordered to be worn always, and in a short time the patient is cured.

Again, very often when the effect of the mydriatic has passed off the patient refuses the cylinder that improved his vision under atropine. He tells you that it makes his vision worse. In spite of this you prescribe it, and—this is a very important point—you insist on the glasses being worn always. He returns in a month or two, assuring you that his headaches have entirely disappeared, that he has become accustomed to the glasses, but that he cannot now see as well without them as he could before using them.

What has happened? At first, when the effect of the mydriatic has passed off, the ciliary muscle returns to its old habit of unequal contraction, and consequently the correcting glasses, instead of helping, make matters worse; but by constantly wearing them the necessity for this unequal contraction disappears, the muscle resumes the normal condition and allows the glasses to do the work. Vision is apparently worse without the glasses because the muscle has forgotten its bad habit; but, of course, like all bad habits, it can be easily re-acquired. The patient has lost nothing but his headache. What stronger proofs could one have that this unequal contraction does occur?

What is more likely to interfere with the nutrition of the

lens than this unequal contraction of the ciliary muscle, producing an artificial lenticular astigmatism, and constantly taking place?

It is interesting to note that in the cases I examined, where the strain was more in one eye than the other, that eye showed greater changes, and in some cases was the only one affected by cataract.

The practical deduction from all this is that by correcting the error of refraction and so removing the strain we ought to be able to arrest or retard the development of cataract, and I fully believe that this is the case. The patients I have under treatment at present most certainly illustrate this, but as the longest period of observation is only four years, the time is at present too short to enable me to use them as convincing proofs of the above theory; time alone will show this, and I shall hope at some future period to bring the subject before you again.

PROPHYLAXIS OF DETACHMENT OF THE RETINA.[1]

No one denies that "prevention is better than cure," and perhaps we never better realise the truth of this old axiom than when we have to deal with diseases which generally lead to death of the individual or of the organ attacked, and whose cure is exceedingly rare. It is too late to think about prevention when the detached retina has been diagnosed by the ophthalmoscope, and therefore it is of the greatest importance that we should recognise the conditions which may lead to this disaster, and see what we can do to prevent it.

Detached retina may be the result of blows on the eye or head, wounds of the eye, or a neoplasm such as sarcoma of the choroid; but I do not intend to deal with these cases here, my remarks being confined entirely to the so-called "idiopathic," or "spontaneous" forms.

The two diseases most commonly associated with this variety of retinal detachment are *myopia* and *cyclitis* (with iritis or choroiditis, or both), and we will now proceed to ascertain whether they stand in the relation of cause to effect, or are merely complications.

What does the pathology of the disease teach us?

---

[1] Read before the West Kent Medico-Chirurgical Society, Dec. 4, 1896.

According to the Leber-Nordenson theory, the following is the sequence of events that leads in the majority of cases, to detached retina :—

Circumscribed inflammation of the anterior portion of the uveal tract and especially the ciliary processes, in other words, cyclitis, or degeneration of the vessels of the uveal tract—leads, in either case, to impairment of the nutrient supply of the vitreous, and this impaired nutrition alters the consistency of the vitreous, producing liquefaction or synchisis, which is almost always followed by shrinking of that body. Now, detachment may occur in several ways. If there has been inflammation of the ciliary region, the contraction of the fibrous tissue drags on the retina and pulls it away from the choroid—this, of course, being specially predisposed to by the lessened support of the shrunken vitreous. Some larger or smaller portion of the retina may refuse to become detached from the choroid, having become adherent through localised retino-choroiditis (Elschnig); a rent then is formed in the retina, and the fluid vitreous at once passes through this rent, and, spreading all over the eye between the retina and the choroid, completes the detachment. Again, a shrinking vitreous alone, will, if adherent wholly or in part to the retina, drag the latter membrane away from the choroid and produce a detachment. Treacher Collins[1] is inclined to support Ræhlmann's view that many cases of spontaneous detachment are due to exudation from the choroidal vessels, the mixing of this exuded serous fluid with the fluid vitreous by a process of diffusion through the retina and a rupture taking place from the tension of the fluid behind the retina.

---

[1] *Trans. Ophth. Soc.*, vol. xvi., p. 81.

In order to thoroughly realise the intimate connection between the retina and the parts composing the uveal tract, it will help us to shortly review what we know of the development of this region of the eye.

The distal wall of the optic cup becomes embryonic retina, and while most of this becomes the true sensory area of the retina, the anterior portion which bends towards the lens, degenerates and is the foundation of the uveal tract (*pars ciliaris retina*). Coincidently with this, the ciliary body and muscle are developed from mesoblastic tissue, the epiblastic vesicle wall and mesoblastic tissue form the iris, and the thinned anterior portion of the vesicle covers the ciliary body, and becoming pigmented, forms the uveal layer at the back of the iris. Now, we see why inflammation of the ciliary region affects the retina, it is really an inflammation of the anterior part of the retina (looked at embryologically), and when contraction takes place here as a result of this inflammation it follows that the retina is dragged away from the choroid, if the inflammation has been severe, or if the vitreous does not lend the normal support. In extreme cases the retina is dragged up into a cord attached to the papilla posteriorly, and passing forwards spreads out like the flower of a convolvulus and is fixed anteriorly at the ora serrata. When we remember that normally the retina is only attached at the papilla and at the ora serrata, and that, in the excised eye, it can be lifted from the choroid with the greatest ease, we can only wonder that detachment does not occur more often. So long as the vitreous remains healthy and of the proper consistency and bulk, so long will it help to keep the retina in its normal position.

In progressive myopia we have often two factors working together to produce detachment, viz., (1) liquefaction of the vitreous, and the shrinking of that body; and (2) lengthening of the antero-posterior axis of the eyeball.

The probable sequence of events is choroiditis (very often accompanied by cyclitis), which is so common in myopia and especially in high myopia, extension of the inflammation into the vitreous, and the subsequent shrinking of that body, and a localised detachment of the retina through the loss of support of the vitreous. At this point the progress of the disease may be arrested, but if not, a rent may be formed in the retina, the fluid vitreous passes through this rent, and spreading all over the eye, makes the detachment universal. Or if we accept Raehlmann's view, the exudation from the choroidal vessels (a sequel of the choroiditis) mixing with the fluid vitreous by diffusion through the retina, a further separation of the retina from the choroid by increase of this subretinal fluid, and finally, possibly a rupture of the retina. Nordenson[1] collecting statistics from various observers, found that out of a total of over 1,100 cases of "spontaneous retinal detachment" myopia was present in 80 per cent. He also states that detachment in myopia occurs late in life, more than 50 per cent. occurring after the fiftieth year.

We can now answer the question we put earlier in the paper, and say definitely that myopia and cyclitis are very potent causes of detachment of the retina, and in their successful treatment lies the prevention of the detachment.

Myopia.—All observers agree that so long as the myopia is progressive the tendency to detachment is present, and the higher the myopia the greater the danger, and that when this progress is arrested the danger is considerably reduced.

---

[1] "Die Netzhautabloesung," 1897.

A full and perfect correction of the error of refraction is the surest method of arresting the progress of myopia. The smallest amount of astigmatism must be recognised, and the myopia should be corrected "*up to the hilt.*"

In all cases a mydriatic should, if possible, be employed, and, as in many cases, the visual acuity is lowered in one or both eyes, we have to depend for the proper estimation of the refraction, almost entirely upon retinoscopy.[1] In young people the glasses representing the full correction of the refractive error should be worn *always*. It is very important that every effort should be made to prevent patients from bringing near work closer to the eye than 33 cms., as we want to avoid, as much as possible, undue convergence; for there is little doubt that the over-used internal recti pulling on the sclerotic tend to lengthen the antero-posterior diameter of the eye, becoming thus a very potent factor in the causation of, or increase of, myopia.

In older patients who have never used glasses for near work, three or four dioptres may have to be deducted for reading, but the full correction should always be given for the distance glasses. In rare cases of very high myopia, we may have to deviate from this rule because the patient refuses to wear the full correction; but as it is in these very cases that detachment is most likely to occur, every effort should be made to induce the patient to consent to the proper treatment.

Following out the idea of reducing convergence strain to the minimum, the most rigid attention should be paid to ophthalmic hygiene. Work that requires close application of the eyes should be continued only for short periods at a time, those periods being divided by outdoor recreation or

---

[1] See p. 138, *et seq.*

exercise. The illumination of the work should be from the side or behind, and never from the front. Very often the foundation of myopia is laid in the schoolroom,—faulty illuminations, faulty desks, and too much book work and writing. It would be well, if we do not want to become a nation of myopes like the Germans, if our schoolmasters would *teach* more—that is, they should explain and impart knowledge by demonstrations and simple lectures, and reduce as much as possible the time spent on "home preparations," which is work done under very great disadvantage, when the brain and eyes are tired, very often by artificial light, and more often than not, when the little worker ought to be in bed.

There are, unfortunately, many cases of high myopia that resist all attempts to arrest their progress, but I believe they are fewer in number than is generally supposed. We must also bear in mind that there is a very great probability that in many of these cases the myopia is not the cause, but one of a number of diseases attacking the eye.[1]

Iritis-cyclitis—Irido-cyclitis. — I have elsewhere[2] expressed my belief that, if an eye is attacked by disease (otherwise than traumatic or infectious) it is an almost sure sign that it has been strained, either through wrong or excessive use, or through some uncorrected error of refraction, which, in the majority of cases, is astigmatism. Just as gout or rheumatism attack an injured joint in preference to a healthy one, just as syphilis commonly chooses a weak spot, so is an eye that has been strained always liable to be attacked by inflammation, and the disease will most probably show itself in that part specially strained. Uncor-

---

[1] Landolt, "Refraction and Accommodation of the Eye," p. 436.
[2] See p. 172, *et seq.*

rected astigmatism must always lead to strain of the ciliary muscle and the door to disease is at once opened.

I am quite sure that cyclitis is a much commoner disease than is supposed, that it is constantly missed, that it is, in a large percentage of cases, caused by astigmatism, and that it is very often the origin of many cases of detached retina that are called "idiopathic."

Whenever any symptom presents itself that suggests that the patient is suffering from eyestrain, such as headache, or blepharitis, &c., the eyes should be put under the influence of a mydriatic, and any error found should be corrected. We shall thus remove the cause which might at any time produce inflammation, which, in its turn, may lead to detachment of the retina.

INDEX.

	PAGE
Accommodation	52
,, amplitude of	53
,, asymmetrical	86
,, influence of age upon	56
,, mechanism of	52
,, punctum proximum of	54
,, punctum remotum of	53
,, and convergence, dissociation between	112
,, ,, relative range of	109
Accommodative asthenopia	51
,, ,, in anisometropia	90
,, ,, in astigmatism	83
,, ,, in hyperopia	72
,, ,, in presbyopia	62
Amplitude of accommodation	53
,, of convergence	106
Anæmia, a cause of eyestrain	40
Anisometropia	89
,, accommodative asthenopia in	90
,, muscular asthenopia in	137
,, treatment of	92
,, unequal accommodation in	90
,, varieties of	89
Asthenopia	
,, accommodative	51
,, astigmatic	83
,, definition of	6
,, differential diagnosis of	30
,, general symptoms of	7
,, history of	1
,, muscular	97
,, neurasthenic	38, 127, 155
,, neuropathic	127, 156
,, reflex	41, 155
,, relation between, and severe neuroses	21
,, relative frequency of	25
,, retinal	151
,, varieties of	6
Astigmatic asthenopia	83, 136
Astigmatism	79
,, causes of	85
,, diagnosis and symptoms of	82
,, hyperopic	86
,, irregular	79
,, myopic	136
,, regular	79

Index.

	PAGE
Astigmatism, seat of	80
,, treatment of	87
,, varieties of	81
Asymmetrical accommodation	86
Binocular vision	102
,, ,, test for	102
Brain disease simulated by asthenopia	30
Centering of glasses	163
Chorea, relation of, to eyestrain	23
Ciliary strain	35
,, ,, causes of	35
,, ,, in ametropia	51
,, ,, in emmetropia	35
Ciliary muscle, spasm of	75
,, ,, unequal contraction of	80
Concentric contraction of visual field	153
Congenital defect of ciliary muscle	41
,, ,, of extrinsic muscles	127
Constipation, a cause of asthenopia	41
Convergence	105
,, amplitude of	106
,, punctum proximum of	108
,, punctum remotum of	107
,, and accommodation, dissociation between	112
,, ,, ,, relative range of	109
Decentering of glasses	137
Definition of eyestrain	6
Differential diagnosis of asthenopia	30
Diplopia	17
Dyerising	49, 128
Dysmenorrhœa, a cause of eyestrain	42
Electric light blindness	159
,, ,, ,, prevention of	162
,, ,, ,, treatment of	162
Epilepsy, relation of, to asthenopia	22
Erythropsia	161
Esophoria	123
Exophoria	121
Eyeball, movements of	98
Eyes, primary position of	103
Eyestrain, *see* Asthenopia	
External recti, insufficiency of	123
Field of vision, concentric contraction of	153
Fusion supplement	111
Glass rod test (Maddox)	104
Headache, ocular	9
,, ,, ætiology and pathology of	13
,, ,, frequency of	12
,, ,, periodic	11
,, ,, position and character of	9
Heterophoria	121
History of eyestrain	1
Hypermetropia, *see* Hyperopia	

	PAGE
Hypermetropic headache	78
Hyperopia	66
,, absolute	71
,, causes of	67
,, facultative	72
,, frequency of asthenopia in	68
,, relative	71
,, treatment of	76
Hyperphoria	124
Influence of age upon accommodation	56
Insomnia caused by eyestrain	21
Insufficiency, muscular	115
,, of external recti	123
,, of internal recti	121
,, of oblique muscles	125
,, of superior and inferior recti	124
,, varieties of	118
Internal recti, insufficiency of	121
Keratoscopy	44
Lactation asthenopia	51
Latent deviation of eyes for distance, test for	104
,, ,, ,, for near point, test for	110
Light, action on the retina of	151
Lightning blindness	161
Maddox tests	104, 110
Megrim	13
,, ophthalmic	15
Metre angle	105
Meridional asymmetrical accommodation	86
Migraine, *see* Megrim	
Muscles of eye, extrinsic	97
Muscular asthenopia	97
,, ,, causes of	126
,, ,, in ametropia	130
,, ,, in anisometropia	137
,, ,, in astigmatism	136
,, ,, in emmetropia	127
,, ,, in hyperopia	130
,, ,, in myopia	131
,, ,, neurasthenic	127
,, ,, neuropathic	127
Muscular insufficiency, *see* Insufficiency	
Mydriasis, a cause of retinal asthenopia	155, 161
Myopia	131
,, asthenopia in	134
,, increased by eyestrain	21
,, treatment of	134
Nasal disease a reflex cause of asthenopia	43
Neuralgia, ocular	9
Neurasthenic asthenopia	38, 127, 155
Neuropathic asthenopia	127, 156
Neuroses, relation between eyestrain and	21
Night-blindness	154, 158

	PAGE
Oblique muscles, insufficiency of	125
Ocular headache, *see* Headache	
Ocular neuralgia	9
Ocular pain	8
Ocular sickness	17
Ocular vertigo	17
Oculo-motor centre	101
Orthophoria	120
Pain, ocular	8
Periodic ocular headache	11
Presbyopia	56
,, causes of	60
,, eyestrain in	62
Primary position of the eyes	103
Prisms	129, 137
Punctum proximum of accommodation	54
,, ,, of convergence	108
Punctum remotum of accommodation	53
,, ,, of convergence	107
Reflex amblyopia	156
Reflex asthenopia	41, 156
Relative range of accommodation and convergence	109
Retina, action of light upon the	151
,, fatigue of, from overuse	155
Retinal asthenopia	151
,, ,, causes of	155
,, ,, neurasthenic	155
,, ,, symptoms of	153
,, ,, treatment of	162
Rhodopsin	151
School desks	47
Sexual abuse, a cause of asthenopia	41, 156
Shadow test	44
Sickness, ocular	17
Smoking, a cause of asthenopia	48
Snellen's coloured glasses	89
Snow blindness	158
Spasm of ciliary muscle	75
Sun blindness	157
Superior rectus, insufficiency of	124
Symptoms, general, of eyestrain	7
Tenotomy	140
Testing the sight, method of	43
Torpor retinæ	151
Traction treatment of insufficiency	130
Unequal accommodation in anisometropia	90
Unequal contraction of ciliary muscle	80, 86
Uric acidæmia	14
Vertigo, ocular	17
Vision, binocular	102
Visual purple	151

OPINIONS OF THE PRESS.

"Apart from all other considerations, Dr. Clarke's monograph is of definite value to those engaged in ophthalmic practice in that the teaching of a large number of scattered writings upon the subject of asthenopia is therein presented, compactly and carefully arranged. The task the author has set himself is no easy one. Asthenopia, especially in reference to its causation, is more protean than most pathological conditions, and a full consideration of it in all its aspects would mean a monstrous work. The difficulties of writing a small book upon a large subject are well known, and the author has surmounted these difficulties very creditably. The book is clearly and pleasantly written, and . . . . has much to commend it."—*British Medical Journal*, June 24th, 1893.

"In this little volume, Dr. Ernest Clarke . . . . has placed the well-known features of excessive work of the eyes, especially in the case of patients who are affected with some error of refraction, or who suffer from muscular or nervous debility, in a clear and easily intelligible form. . . . . This little monograph upon an important subject has been well thought out and well written by the author."—*Lancet*, Jan. 7th, 1893.

"The treatment of Eyestrain is very sensibly discussed, and much stress is laid on the proper observance of truly hygienic habits, both in work and relaxation. . . . . The book is well arranged and carefully edited, and is a very useful addition to the literature of Ophthalmology."—*The Medical Magazine*, Feb., 1893.

"The author of this well-printed monograph has done good service in collecting, digesting, and reproducing, in a very readable form, all that is known about this important and interesting subject."—*The Dublin Journal of Medical Science*, Dec., 1892.

"This small handbook will be found of value to all practitioners who may be called upon to treat cases of frontal neuralgia or headache, as well as to ophthalmic surgeons. Much of what has been written on the symptoms of Eyestrain is referred to and elaborated. Various forms of asthenopia—accommodative, muscular, and retinal—are described and explained. Refractive errors, neuroses, and muscular insufficiencies and anomalies are fully considered, together with their treatment by lenses, prisms, or operation. The index to the book and the references to authors show that the writer has not taken any narrow view of his subject."—*The Bristol Medico-Chirurgical Journal*, June, 1893.

"The book shows its author to be a man of most persevering research, and may be said to contain an exceedingly good summation of our present state of knowledge on this important condition. We congratulate the author on the portion of his book which deals with muscular asthenopia. In our opinion . . . . it is excellent."—*The Glasgow Medical Journal*, Feb., 1893.

www.ingramcontent.com/pod-product-compliance
Lightning Source LLC
Chambersburg PA
CBHW032227230426
43666CB00033B/1623